STRIKE ACROSS THE EMPIRE

STRIKE ACROSS THE EMPIRE

The Seamen's Strike of 1925: in Britain, South Africa and Australasia

Baruch Hirson

and

Lorraine Vivian

Clio Publications

London

First published in 1992 by
Clio Publications
c/o 13 Talbot Avenue
London N2 OLS

© Baruch Hirson and Lorraine Vivian, 1992

ISBN 1 897640 00 5

Typeset by Voluntary Labour
Printed and bound in Great Britain by UTL, London

Cover picture: BritishSeamen marching to jail in Wellington, September 1925.
— Courtesy, National Maritime Museum, Greenwich

Preface

This essay provides the first account of the one international strike in history: that of the British seamen in 1925. Starting soon after the 1st of August in Britain, the strike failed to gain momentum until seamen walked off the ships three weeks later in Australia, New Zealand and South Africa.

The seamen stayed out for over three months in Australia and for about two months elsewhere. They defied the governments of four countries, the most powerful cartel of the time (that of the shipowners) and their union in Britain. Yet except for a number of student dissertations dealing with local events the history of this strike has not been told.

William Beinart, a South African historian, took one of the authors of this essay (Baruch Hirson) to meet Solomon Biurski, a veteran member of the Communist Party of South Africa, in London in 1984. Beinart had a copy of Biurski's unpublished autobiography in which he claimed that in 1925 he had organized and led the committeei supporting the striking seamen in Cape Town. The story, as told by Biurski, was riveting but also puzzling: there was no record of the event in any history of South Africa. Neither Beinart nor Hirson had heard of this before and, in a preliminary search for evidence of the event, no references to the strike were found in the popular histories of trade unionism in Britain. At a later date, a more thorough search revealed some short accounts, most of them confined to events in Britain or Australuia.

Beinart, although interested, felt that it was too far from his existing research interests. Hirson, left with the matter in his hands, turned to the newspaper section of the British Library to check Biurski's story. What he found was remarkable. For almost two months the strike was on the main news pages, and Biurski's activities, although not quite as described in the manuscript, figured prominently. The Cape Town newspapers also referred to activities in Durban and had items from Australia, New Zealand and Britain. This initiated a search over many months through newspapers that were available in the British newspaper library, and the story grew.

Yet no documents referring to the strike were found in the British Public Records Office. Even the papers of the Seamen's Union, available at Warwick University, contained few documents for the year 1925. Of all the main British actors only George Hardy wrote about the event. Emanuel Shinwell, leader of a rival union, which was involved in the strike, avoids the year 1925 in the many versions of his autobiography. The official and unofficial histories of the Communist Party in Great Britain, and the autobiographies of persons connected with the National Minority Movement (such as Harry Pollit), made no mention of the strike.

An extensive correspondence with friends and academics led to new contacts in Australia and New Zealand and this yielded further information, copies of debates in the Australian parliament and senate, and also some archival sources in libraries. The research was revealing on several counts. Firstly for the wealth of newspaper coverage, from all sides of the political spectrum — although there were some newspapers which we sought to no avail. Secondly for the repeated assertion that it was a communist plot to destabilize the British empire, or the governments of one or other of the countries involved. Thirdly for the racial over-tones that were implicit (or explicit) in many of the arguments in Britain, South Africa and Australia. But over and above these factors it became apparent that there was a malaise in the seamen's unions and in the British Trade Union Congress. Havelock Wilson and his lieutenants in the seamen's union in Britain con-trolled the union with little regard for the membership and in their actions used methods that could be described as near fascist. Indeed Edward Tupper, one of Wilson's cohorts, subsequently wrote of using his 'storm troopers' in organizing a race riot. The leader of the seamen's union in Australia, ostensibly radical in 1925, subsequently joined ranks with Wilson in a rightward move that led him to con-demn socialism and champion a 'white Australia' policy. The TUC, in the months before the General Strike, stood by supinely and refused assistance to the striking men. They reaped the 'reward' for their inactivity in 1926 when, during the General Strike, which revolved around the action of the coal miners, the seamen were forced to bring in cargo loads of coal.

This meant that a crucial event in the months leading up to the strike of 1926, and one which had a crippling effect on the miners' action, has been overlooked. What started as a search to confirm a claim in a participant's memoir became a search for the understanding the first shot of the General Strike and posed a question that was always present, but has not been answered: was the seamen's strike of 1925 provoked in order to undermine the seamen before the main action was played out?

The reading of newspapers was more than one person could encompass. For-tunately, two students at the Middlesex Polytechnic, who attended courses given by Hirson, offered their assistance and went through the tedious task of searching through newspapers and journals: Clare Ghazi–Horsiny and Lorraine Vivian. After graduating, Vivian was persuaded by Hirson to undertake research on the strike in Britain for a Master's degree at Warwick University. For over a year this involved a separation of interests. In order to satisfy academic criteria, Lorraine worked independently, maintaining only minimum contact with Hirson. Only after she had graduated was it possible to resume collaboration.

By this time Hirson had completed his reading on the rise and decline of the strike outside Britain. Using the material in Vivian's dissertation, the work was written by Hirson. Both names appear on the title page because of the work that has been put into this research.

Now that our study of the strike has been taken as far as seems possible, we turn once again to the vexed question of the absence of the strike in most histories of trade unionism. We have to ask whether the seamen's strike was overshadowed by the general strike of 1926. But this makes no sense: the events of 1925 fed into the strike of 1926. Wherever we looked it seemed that almost all the major actors in the events of 1925 had something to hide: the communists because of the collapse of the Anglo–Soviet agreement in 1926; the Trade Union Congress because it had refused to support the seamen in 1925; Shinwell because of his tardy and confusing actions during the strike; and the officials of the National Union of Seamen and Firemen in 1925 had more to conceal than we could uncover six decades later.

While it always remains possible that failure to discuss the strike has been an oversight, it seems more likely that the open antagonism to the strike by the official union and the failure of the TUC to lend support to the seamen has led to its relative neglect in Britain. The failure to see the connection between the strike of 1925 and that of 1926 is, in our opinion, a major failure of the histories written to commemorate the General Strike.

In South Africa the immaturity of history as a discipline and the relative newness of labour history is sufficient to explain its absence from history books. Australia has several accounts of the strike in the ports, and some dissertations written for degree purposes in the universities. Most of these are not available to outside readers.

Having completed the work we were more than surprised when told by some publishers that the book was not viable because it was not 'reader specific'. That is, the potential readership was too scattered to warrant publication. Other publishers were less complimentary and this persuaded us to try our own publishing facilities.

Hirson did the typesetting and the design and got the copy camera–ready for the printer. It now remains to be seen whether there is a reading public out there, willing to read a story that we think compelling and important.

We thank the many people who assisted us in the Bibliography, leaving only our respective families to thank. They rendered every assistance while we took off time to work at the history. Without their forbearance this work would never have been completed. If we have erred at any point they, and the many people who have assisted us, are certainly not responsible.

Baruch Hirson
Lorraine Vivian

CONTENTS

The Strike Across the Empire   **1**

     Sailors with 'Blank Faces'   2

1. Background to a Strike   **7**

     Britain in the Post–War World   7
     The British Merchant Fleet   10
     The Money Crisis in Britain   12

2. The Seafarers and Their Organisation   **13**

     Put the £1 in the Plate   13
     First Steps in Organising the Firemen and Seamen   17
     Recognition and a Split   19
     The War, and a National wage Agreement   19
     The Amalgamated Marine Workers Union   20
     Control of the Seamen's Union   23
     The Voice of the Seamen   25

3. The Strike Begins in Britain   **27**

     Prelude to the General Strike   27
     The National Minority Movement   28
     The Move to Strike Action   29
     The AMWU Backs the Strike   32
     Dissension over Tactics   34
     The View from the 'Top'   35

4. Racism and the Sailor   **37**

     White Sailor vs Black   37
     The Background of Rioting   39
     Coloured crews in the 1925 Strike   41

5. Solidarity Abroad   **43**

     The Dispute Aboard the SS Inkum   43
     The Threat of Deportation   44
     The Strike in Durban   47

6. All Out in Australia   **51**

     The One Hundred and Two Days   51
     The First Negotiations   53
     Stalemate on the Waterfront   55
     Caring for the Strikers   56
     Violence in the Closing Stages   59
     The Cost of the Strike   62

7. The Strike in South Africa   **64**

The Pact:Government and the Strike   64
The Strike Spreads to Cape Town   65
The End of the Road   67
A Labour 'Coup' and the End of the Strike   69
The Impact on South Africa   70

8. The 'Homeboat' Strike   **72**

The Strike in New Zealand   72
The Support Committees   75
'Victims of Wilson's Treachery'   77
The Cost of the Strike to New Zealand   77

9. The Strike Grinds Down   **81**

'The Scab on the Ocean Wave'   81
Poverty and the Board of Guardians   83
The Men Go Back   85
The Wireless Operators   87
The Price they Paid   88

10. Strike Against the Tide   **90**

References   **95**

Bibliography   **107**

Index   **113**

Abbreviations Used In The Book

AMWU	Amalgamated Marine Workers Union
AWCT	Association of Wireless and Cable Telegraphists
BSU	British Seafarers Union
CPA	Communist Party of Australia
CPGB	Communist Party of Great Britain
CPSA	Communist Party of South Africa
CSC	Central Strike Committee
FSU	Federated Seaman's Union (of Australia)
ICU	Industrial and Commercial Workers of Africa
IFTW	International Federation of Transport Workers
LPA	Labor Party of Australia
MRC	Modern Research Centre
NMB	National Maritime Board
NMM	National Minority Movement
NSFU	National Sailors' and Fireman's Union
PC5	Port Clearance Card
RILU	Red International of Labour Unions (Profintern)
SAIC	South African Indian Congress
SALP	South African Labour Party
TUC	Trades Union Congress

INTRODUCTION

The Strike Across the Empire

At the beginning of August 1925 the wage of British seamen was cut by 10 percent. The most galling features of this reduction was the role of J Havelock Wilson, the President of the National Sailors and Firemen's Union of Great Britain and Ireland (NSFU). Without consulting the seamen he had offered the reduction to the employers. Consequently the strike that followed was as much against the union's leaders as against the shipowners.

The £1 reduction imposed on the seamen, with the connivance of their union leaders, was an act of betrayal. The British trade unions had just rejected the government's call for a general reduction of wages and, in concerted action, had threatened to call a general strike. They had won and wages were left untouched. July 31st, the deadline for the cut, was celebrated by the trade unions as *Red Friday* to mark their victory. Yet within forty-eight hours, seamen seeking a berth had to accept a wage cut. In the midst of their jubilations, few workers stopped to pause at the humiliation of the nation's seamen.

During the government's campaign to lower wages, the shipowners had joined the general clamour and, to the chagrin of all seafarers, had found willing allies in their trade union officials. They had been betrayed by their own association and, furthermore, they were obviously vulnerable. There was large scale unemployment in the merchant marine and crews could be brought in from idle ports by the larger shipping lines. The seamen also faced competition from Lascars (Indian) and Chinese sailors. This alternative work force was paid at appreciably lower rates and that, whether intended or not, gave rise to strong racial antagonisms, a factor that was also to play an important part in the events that followed.

The seamen who did come out on strike when the cut was announced in Britain faced insuperable difficulties. The NSFU condemned those who would not sail and assisted the shipowners in recruiting scabs. The seamen were also split, occupationally, regionally and politically, and that was a barrier to organizational coherence both at home and at sea. Nor were they all in the same union. The Amalgamated Marine Workers Union (AMWU) led by Emanuel (Manny) Shinwell and smaller groups such as the Association of Wireless and Cable Telegraphists had emerged historically out of sectional unions. The AMWU leaders, irrevocably split themselves, breathed hot and cold throughout August 1925 before declaring their support for the strike and even then they failed to offer a decisive lead.

The seamen's strike was not foreseen by the trade union movement in Britain nor offered support when it broke out. The Trades Union Congress (TUC) rejected all appeals for assistance and refused to support the strike because if was 'unofficial'. It was left to the National Minority Movement (NMM)[1] to organise the unofficial strike committee in London. Perhaps it was this cold-shouldering of the strike that has led to its exclusion from most analyses of trade union activities Yet our investigation led us to believe that the defeat of the seamen's strike contributed to the collapse of the General Strike only nine months later.[2]

By mid-August the seamen's strike had all but collapsed in Britain. Most ships had sailed with a full complement of men and there seemed little purpose in the small handful of strikers in British ports persisting. It was at this juncture that the nature of the strike altered. After 20 August, when the ships reached ports in Australia, New Zealand and South Africa, men declared that they would not sail again. For the next sixty to one hundred days British ships were immobilised.

The impact on the three Dominions in which the strike was effective, even if eventually the men were forced back, was more diverse. In Australia, and to a lesser degree New Zealand, the antagonisms between trade unionists and government intensified. In South Africa it undoubtedly started the rift in the all-white Labour Party and distanced it from the National Party, its partner in the government. In all of them the economies were badly affected.

A strike in 1925 was a serious matter for the economies of Britain and the Dominions. Air travel, which was to change the relationship between Europe and the rest of the world within a decade, was still in its infancy and exporters of raw materials, agricultural produce and manufactured goods relied on regular sailings, as did mail and travellers, tourists and immigrants. Any prolonged delay could lead to severe losses for farmers, traders and manufacturers, as well as considerable inconvenience for those who maintained contact with persons overseas.

The shipowners were fully aware of the role they played in transporting people and in keeping international trade alive, but their first concern was the maintenance of a healthy balance sheet. The world-wide cartel, in which British owned ships played a central role, had plans to reduce costs to maintain (and improve) its profitability. In the process they were prepared for a large initial drop in profits if that was the price to be paid for controlling their crews.

The employers would have had their way within weeks if it had not been for the action of the thousands of men who walked off the ships in the ports of South Africa and Australasia. With the men and women of the Dominions who supported them, they kept the strike alive. It was only when the seamen in South African ports, despairing of victory, decided to sail again that the AMWU called off the strike in Britain. One week later the NMM-controlled Central Strike Committee with headquarters in London conceded defeat.

Sailors with 'Blank Faces'

The decision to cut the wages in August 1925 was the cruellest cut of the time: both absolutely, in view of the low wage earned by the seamen, and relatively when compared to the income earned by the shipowners. The wages paid to seamen had risen to an average of £14 10s per month after the war, but these rates had been pared back to £9 in four cuts (50s in May 1921, 30s and then 10s in March and May 1922, and a further 20s in May 1923). Wages then rose marginally to £10 per month in 1924. However, the average wage was reduced by the loss of wages when the ship was in port and the seaman's family survived only by drawing on social benefit.

The peculiar way in which the wages were reduced in 1925 is discussed in the next chapter. What concerns us here is its impact on the seamen at the time. A steward told his story to a reporter during the strike:

Q: Do you find it hard to live on the present wage?

A: Exceedingly hard, but it would be much worse with the £1 per month reduction ... the wages of a steward under the proposed reduction would be £8 5s. per month. I am in the habit of allowing 30s per week to my wife. This sum is paid fortnightly ... [and] in order that my wife may live for the first fortnight I draw an advance of £3.

The voyages to Australia and back usually take three and a half months ... For the ... voyage I would receive in wages £28 17s 6d. First of all there is the £3 in advance; there are then seven allotments of £3 per fortnight ... £1 must be paid for unemployment and national health insurance. That is compulsory... It is impossible for a man to avoid some small expenditure: such things as tobacco and other incidentals. Put that down as £1 for the trip... Now without expending one half-penny on myself for clothing and enjoyment I would have between £2 and £3 to draw when I was paid off in London. [The union officials] will be waiting to claim another pound for union dues. As a rule a ship is laid up for about three weeks in London, and for two weeks of that time I am unemployed ...

Q: Well, how do you and your family manage to live?

A: The majority of the lower paid men on British vessels when in London go on the dole right away. They are compelled to do this: it is the only possible way they have of living until they sign on a vessel again. I may say that several of the men on British ships today receive Poor Law relief. The wage today [before the cut] is not sufficient to purchase the requirements for themselves and their families.

He later repeated that there were seamen in regular employment on British ships who received Poor Law relief. The shipowners were being effectively subsidised by the poor law relief authorities.[3]

The Rev J S Hart, Anglican Dean of Melbourne, appalled by the evidence, was quoted as saying:

To say that the shipping industry cannot stand [higher wages] is nonsense. If it can stand 'luxury ships', and pay good dividends on a heavily watered capital, it can do simple justice to its employees. Shipowners are not looked upon as a very poverty-stricken class, and nowadays they have abolished competition, and, having a monopoly, can make their charges sufficient to cover all fair expenses. If they are prevented from amassing fortunes, who cares?[4]

The seafarers thought likewise and, after walking off their ships, established links with local seamen or trade unions, with socialist and communist groups, and with the unofficial strike committee that had been set up in London. The only weapon against an international combine was international action and, whether aware of this or not, the British seamen started one of the few strikes of the twentieth century to have international dimensions.

The strike was about a wage cut but the seamen complained about their working and living conditions as well. On a voyage the seaman would get food and he had a place to sleep. However he had little else. The Committee of Overseas Seamen in New Zealand said in their 'Strike Bulletin' No 2 that when they signed on they were among the lowest paid (white) workers in the world, 'engaged in a perilous occupation'. They continued:

> After working between 70 to 80 hours per week, and living and eating in a dark, badly-ventilated fo'c's'le, we receive the sum of £2.5s per week ... Out of this ... we are forced to buy our own eating utensils, bed and blankets, towel and soap, pay 5d per week to a national health insurance, and 9d per week to an unemployed assurance.

Conditions were described by the Strike Committee in Australia as hellish. In a message printed in the *WorkersWeekly they wrote:*

> Some of the ships we sail in are lousy, and there is nothing done. Fumigation does not kill the lice. We eat and sleep in the same room and at all hours we are called upon to do anything whether we are wet through or not — there is nowhere to dry our clothes and this necessitates at least four changes of clothing, and on £9 ... where are we going to get them — no we're mostly wet. Its hell — we tell you the conditions of living in British ships and as to shore leave. It remains at the discretion of the captain whether we get leave or not. If we overstay our leave we are logged and leave the ship with a bad discharge for even a trivial offence such as this, and a bad discharge may mean that our living is taken from us.[5]

Generalizations about seafarers conditions are difficult but for all of them work was arduous and dangerous, the working hours unsociable, the incidence of accidents and disease higher than average. Speaking about conditions in New Zealand, Olssen said the seamen 'worked and lived under a tightly organized system of command, disobedience being fraught with severe penalties'. Yet, he said, this was too vague a profile. Seamen had their own groupings on the ships and although they could, and did, unite at times, they reacted differently to the problems they faced. Firemen and stokers, he said, formed 'clannish and stroppy groups' and did not play much part in trade union affairs. For the rest, much depended on the size of the ship and the variety of men employed: the deck was 'a complex world of bosuns, lamptrimmers, watchmen, donkeymen, stokehold hands, firemen, and seamen'. There were also the cooks, stewards, and other hands that made up this floating island — tied together for several months, and then often splintered and dispersed after they docked.[6] For the historian their faces are blank and even the press photographs of the time fail to fill in the details — but they were reported to have marched and stood together against the greatest odds. Many were radicalized during the strike and although they originally marched to patriotic war-time tunes, ended by marching (at least in the Dominions) to the strains of the 'Red Flag'. However, many seamen — and their supporters — spoke contemptuously of the coloured races. This was compounded by an ubiquitous racism that was thoughtlessly absorbed, if not welcomed, by most workers and the genuine fear that foreign labour would be used to cut wages. This helped fuel the anti-Chinese and anti-black riots in British ports in 1911 and 1919.

In Australia, seamen faced competition from poorly paid Asian labour and, although a few realized that the answer was to unionize all seafarers, most supported a 'White Australia' policy, denigrating all blacks and Asians. On the eve of the British seamen's strike, the *Australasian Seamen's Journal* (Vol 8, No 53), published an article compounded of poor anthropology and outright prejudice, which claimed that capitalism had 'forced the pace', advancing humanity to its present position, but,

... the capitalist class has built colossal fortunes out of cotton and sugar plantations, worked by enforced negro labour, when we know that, if left alone, these workers would be still lying in the sun the greater part of the time, feeding themselves on the banana with which Nature has provided them. The mine magnates of South Africa forced the Kaffirs to live in compounds and to toil on the mines to make profits for them, but when these men return to their distant kraals, they go back, willingly, to the simplest way of existence.

In India millions of poor peasants, producing almost incredible fortunes for their native and British rulers, if left alone would return thanks for a mud hut, a handful of rice, a cotton garment — and peace.

Perhaps aware of the overtones in his article, the writer added:

Even in Western countries there are millions of poor workers, operating industries which bring the greatest luxury to the owning class, who do not KNOW that their houses are hovels; that their clothes are rags; that their children ought not to toil in factories, but should be in school, and that they themselves are starved and ignorant.

This account of conditions in India is absurd and it is noteworthy that there was no suggestion that the 'ignorant' white workers would gladly retire to eat 'bananas' (or fish and chips?) or return to 'their simple ways of existence', whatever that implied.

When the strike was over those who returned to the UK faced unemployment. Others stayed behind in the Dominions but most were denied entry to the local seamen's union, lest it lead to a surplus of men in a decreasing labour market and depress wages. By a twist of fate, the British seamen were placed in the same position as coloured workers, despite the solidarity accorded them during the long strike. What happened to those who stayed in the Dominions is not recorded, and they seem to have found jobs in other occupations. Many showed qualities of leadership during the strike. How much of this was fed into the workers' movement in the coming grim period of defeats and economic destitution remains unknown. What can be told is the story of their resolution, their initiative and their determination. If there were faults in the conduct of the strike, these are easily discernible, but over and above any mistakes the seamen and their supporters provide a remarkable demonstration of international working class solidarity.

Of the women who waited at home for the seamen to return, there are only the scantiest of details. The wages (or 'allotments') due to families of men on strike were stopped by the shippers at an early stage of the action. Subsequently, many wives were reduced to absolute destitution. Some despaired and fell back on friends and families but many, used to privation at the best of times, demonstrated in support of the strike, protested at the plight of their families and set up groups for joint action. Others wrote despairingly to their men abroad, recounting the misery to which they and their children were reduced. The plight of these families, only partially told in the local and national press, was not very different from families split apart during war — except that in this case the women could not look to any official body for sympathy. Neither state, employer nor trade union movement was prepared to assist the families of men on strike. If anything, the plight of these dependents was used as yet another lever to force the men to return to work at the lower wage.

The strikers went back defeated and yet this was an important event on two accounts. Firstly, it was one of the few strikes that stretched across the seas, providing an example of class solidarity that transcended national boundaries. Secondly, this was a strike in which many communists were involved: in Britain in the strike committee; in Australia and New Zealand, because some leaders of the national seamen's union were in the Communist Party and in South Africa, because leading communists offered support to the seamen. Yet much of this was fortuitous: there was no concerted communist campaign. S P Bunting, the South African delegate to the Sixth Congress of the Communist International in 1928 complained in public session that throughout the strike there had been no advice or instructions from communists in Europe, and the local party had been left to take decisions by itself.

1

BACKGROUND TO A STRIKE

The intention of the capitalists of this country were made perfectly clear by Mr Baldwin when he stated that the workers of this country have got to have reductions of wages to help put industry on its feet, and in this view he is supported by men like Mr Havelock Wilson, who has recently been successful in reducing the wages of the seamen at the instigation of the shipowners.

Marine Worker, September 1925[1]

Britain in the Post-War World

The editors of the *Marine Worker*, organ of the Amalgamated Marine Workers Union (AMWU), were bitterly opposed to the official seamen's union, the National Union of Seamen and Firemen of Ireland and Great Britain (NSFU), its leadership and, in particular, Havelock Wilson, the president of the union.

Editorial comments in the magazine were directed at the trade union movement at large and their attack linkedon the official union with the government for its offensive against existing wage agreements. On 30 June 1925 the mine owners, backed by the government, had given one month's notice that their 1921 agreement with the Miner's Federation of Great Britain would be terminated; that wages in the coal mines would be reduced by 10–25 per cent, and that the national minimum wage would be ended after 31 July. The mine owners claimed that this was made necessary by their losses over the past year and this alarmed trade union leaders of the steel workers, foundry workers, electrical trades and others as a threat to the wages in their own trades. The trade unions united and a special conference of the Trades Union Congress agreed that a strike would be declared on midnight of Friday, 31 July. In face of this threat the government, which had not yet completed its anti-strike strategy, offered to subsidise the miners' wages. The strike was called off and the Labour movement spoke jubilantly of *Red Friday*.[2] But the celebrations were premature — the reductions had only been delayed. Nine months later wages were cut and the government was in position to defeat the workers when they came out on strike.

But was it true that wages had to be cut to put Britain 'back on its feet'? The decline in Britain's hegemonic position in the world was already apparent before 1914. Facing competition from America and Germany, Britain was no longer supreme among industrial powers and the upshot had been economic stringency and increased class battles in the years before the outbreak of war.[3] As a result, said Trotsky, 'there had been unparalleled class battles waged by mine workers, railroad workers and the transport workers in general'.

The war of 1914–18 interrupted this revolutionary process and stopped the growth of the strike wave. Ending in the destruction of Germany, it seemed to restore to England the role of world hegemony. But it soon became apparent that instead of retarding the decline of England, the war had actually accelerated its decline . . .

During the war, the enormous economic preponderance of the United States was developed and revealed in its full proportions. The emergence of that country from the stage of an overseas' provincialism suddenly forced Great Britain into second place.

At the conclusion of the First World War, Britain had hoped to stand at the head of Europe and once more to be the colossus of the world. The British ruling class stood aloof from Europe and, by virtue of its colonial possessions, still aspired to leadership of the West. Germany, its rival in Europe, had been defeated and, it was hoped, relegated to second class status through the Treaty of Versailles and the retribution exacted on her by reparations. However, states had emerged to displace Britain from the centre of the stage. To the east lay Japan, a new power to be reckoned with, although not yet an economic giant and to the west lay the United States, to which all Europe was directly or indirectly indebted.

The war, confidently expected to be over in months, dragged on for four long years and the continent was torn apart — as men were slaughtered in the trenches of Flanders and the ragged battles on the eastern front. Of the 60 million men mobilized by both sides in the war, over eight million were killed in the battlefields, seven million permanently disabled, and a further fifteen million more or less seriously injured. In the light of these global figures, Britain's losses were modest. Nonetheless, some 745,000 men and women were killed and 1.6 million wounded.[4] Then came the influenza epidemic of 1918–19 in which many more died.

The war destroyed resources and devastated the fields of Europe. Worse was to follow. Tsarist Russia was replaced by a Bolshevik regime, which, weak as it was, became the 'spectre that haunted Europe', while the break-up of the Austro-Hungarian and Ottoman Empires created new crises in Europe. Only the empires of Britain and France seemed to remain intact, and even strengthened by the acquisition of Germany's former possessions. Yet this too was an illusion. The colonial peoples were already stirring and new struggles pointed to the breaking of imperial control. Before that happened there were new factors loosening the ties between metropolis and colony. Among these was the altered balance of forces on the seas. In the same essay Trotsky pointed to the vital connection:

The commercial, industrial, and naval hegemony of England has in the past almost automatically assured the bonds between the various portions of the empire. The New Zealand minister, Reeves, wrote before 1900: 'two things maintain the present relation of the colonies with England: first their faith in the generally peaceful intentions of England's policy; second, their faith in England's rule of the seas'. Of course the decisive factor is the second. The loss of hegemony of the seas proceeds parallel with the development of the centrifugal forces within the empire. The preservation of the empire is more and more threatened by the diverging interests of the dominions and the struggles of the colonies.

The victorious powers took steps to protect their hegemony by expropriating a large proportion of the German navy after the war. But that was at best a temporary expedient and ignored the existence of a world-wide shipping combine.

Imperial connections placed British shipowners in the fore in protecting national al shipping routes yet these men were not averse to dividing the world with their European 'competitors', were quite willing to use European shipyards to build their ships and to employ 'foreign' seamen to cut their wages bill. They also came out of the war considerably richer than when they went in. Figures widely quoted from Sir Leo Chiozza Money during the seamen's strike of 1925 stated that:

In the first 31 months of the war, before the excess profits tax came into operation, the shipowners of the British Isles made, in actual profits £350,000,000, and the ships had increased in value – not in number – from ... [£170,000,000] to £500,000,000.[5]

This is only part of the story. We will return to the shipping companies and their vessels below.

The war was followed, mainly in Britain and the USA, by a spending spree, based on the demand for commodities that had been so scarce during the war. Aldcroft, the economic historian, is quoted as saying that this fuelled a boom, helped on by a shortage of shipping space and a dislocation of internal transport systems in the immediate post-war period.[6] This was inflationary. Within the year the stock markets collapsed and the boom was over. Exports and prices fell equally sharply, shipping declined and unemployment rose rapidly.

Individual capitalists (and combines) had emerged from the war greatly enriched. They flourished in the post-war boom but felt the squeeze when the economy went into recession. This was also a period of stringency for the government ment as revenue fell with declining trade. Also, as a consequence of war-time borrowing, Great Britain was deeply indebted to the United States and beholden to her in the finance market. Although European states were in turn indebted to Britain, they could not, or would not, pay: while Britain was pledged to honour her war debts. According to Palme Dutt, theoretician of the Communist Party of Great Britain (CPGB), Britain lost markets as a result of the war. By 1925 exports had fallen to 75 per cent of its pre-war volume, while exports from America and some European states expanded. This led to an increase of Britain's balance of trade deficit from £134m in 1913, to £212m in 1923 and £344m in 1924. Capital for new investment abroad declined dramatically, approaching zero in 1925.[7] The employers found a simple solution for ending this decline: wages had to be cut and by 1925 the national wages bill was reduced to approximately one-half of its 1920 level. This was achieved in three cuts: £6,000,000 in the weekly full-time wages of 7.25 million wage workers in 1921, a further £4,200,000 a week affecting 7.5 million in 1922, and about £500,000 a week inflicted on three million workers in 1923. But the effect of these cuts was disastrous: the loss of purchasing power on the home market leading to further reductions in trade and industry.[8]

Nonetheless dividends in Britain were kept high: average payment on ordinary shares of 1,400 companies rose from 8.6 in 1922, to 9 (1923), 9.5 (1924) and 10.5 per cent (first quarter of 1925). Net profits rose as wages were cut, from £80m in 1922 to £115m in both 1923 and 1924.[9] In his article, Dutt maintained that:

> ...there is a real meaning behind the talk of 'bankruptcy', and a real force which drives inevitably to the present offensive. The fear is not yet the fear of 'bankruptcy' or 'starvation'. But it is the fear of the loss of that predominant position in the world market and in world finances which is the necessary basis of British Imperialism.
> The continuance of the Empire structure depends on the continual provision of fresh supplies of capital [for] foreign investment. If this dwindles, the colonies drop off and pass elsewhere. On this basis is built the vastly inflated structure of exporting industries, to the exclusion of vital home needs such as housing.

The mixed fortunes of the mercantile marine, this once mighty arm of British supremacy and control of the empire, was central to Britain's continued decline in the inter-war years.

The British Merchant Fleet

The lines of communication between the British Isles and the rest of the world devolved on the navy and the mercantile fleet. In wartime it was the navy that protected the country and it was the seamen who ensured the continuation of supplies, of armaments and of merchandise. Because of her pre-war supremacy, Britain possessed some 42 per cent of the world's ocean-going steamer tonnage and about 60 per cent of the world's shipbuilding capacity in 1914.[10] This was deemed sufficient to allow for the maintenance of naval supremacy during the war, but the U–Boats had sunk a total of 1.7 million gross tons of British shipping by August 1916. The destruction intensified until the navy f was able to counter the German naval offensive. By the end of the war Britain alone had lost one out of every four ships that put to sea, that is, about 7.75 million tons, yet the shipowners still prospered. At the end of 1916, after an outcry over profiteering, the government appointed a Controller of Shipping, but controls never covered all the ships. Each year the total tonnage of shipping rose, much of it requisitioned by the government to bring in crucial war goods. Consequently, 'Profits soared, and large capital gains were registered in mergers and purchases'.[11]

Between 17 and 20,000 men of the merchant marine went down with their ships but their employers profited, being paid handsome compensation for every ship sunk at sea. In this most patriotic of wars, Lloyd George had spoken of a 'land fit for heroes' and, in recognition of their contribution to the war effort, seamen had been extolled as 'heroes', a fact they referred to bitterly when they were charged and sent to prison during the strike of 1925.

British shipping companies went through a lean period — or at least a period in which the rich war-time profits could not be sustained. In part, this was a consequence of the depressed state of world trade in which too many ships chased decreasing freight, but there were other factors that led to this drop in profitability. The British shipowners had either taken possession of aged German ships, or bought a large number of craft at inflated prices after the war[12] and, with a large surplus of boats on their hands, were less willing than some of their competitors in Europe to convert to cost-saving oil-firing or diesel motors. The surfeit of boats, the drop in trade and the imposition of quotas by the US, the dramatic drop in emigration — a drop of 217,041 passengers between 1923 and 1924[13] — all affected the shipping lines. Freight dropped from an index of 374 in 1920 to 166 in 1921, and tramp freights from 602 (1920) to 141 (1921), both declining further, if more slowly, through the 1920s.[14]

The effect of the recession on dividends is a matter of dispute. Trade unionists maintained that the British shipowners were part of the richest combine in the world, had made £350m profit during the war (greater than the registered value of all the ships in the world), and continued to make handsome profits. They quoted W T R Preston, who reported in February 1925 to the Canadian government that an international shipping combine had divided the world into 'spheres of influence'. It raised fares exorbitantly and threatened competitors with ruin. The combine met regularly in Paris, Brussels, Vienna or Berlin, but not in Britain, 'to avoid complications with British authorities' and he added:

This combine is interlocked with the great steamship lines plying between the European continent and South America, South Africa, India, Australia and New Zealand ...
The British steamship interests control not only the North Atlantic steamship traffic, but exercise a predominating influence in the great world-wide steamship combine.[15]

From 1911 to 1925, freight rates from Montreal to Britain increased by 700 per cent, said Preston, until competition from independent companies cut the increases to 50 per cent. Consequently, under monopoly control, Canadian exporters lost millions of dollars annually and the export trade to Britain was almost extinguished. Furthermore 'excess' profits on emigration to Canada during 1919–24 had been £43m. Summing up, he said

The moving spirits in this gigantic world-wide maritime organization had conspired, combined, agreed and arranged to unduly limit the facilities of ocean transportation, and cause serious oppression to individuals, and incalculable injury to the general public.

Similarly, a Navigation Commission investigated the Australian Shipping monopoly, and Frank Anstey, a Labour Party member of the House of Representatives, submitted a supplementary memorandum to the Governor–General. He said many alleged Australian companies were in fact British, but 'acted under aliases as if they were criminals seeking to escape attention'. Consequently, the passenger trade, which was nominally confined to locally registered companies, was carried by British interests alone. Even the sea tramps, that carried all the coastal cargo trade, were auxiliaries to the combine, and regulated their rates to ensure that there was no competition.[16]

The routes between England and the Pacific Ocean were dominated by the Peninsula and Oriental Shipping Company (P&O), and its major shareholder, Lord Inchcape, was seen by the left to typify the combine. The *Westralian Worker* of 11 September 1925 said that he was also a director of the Anglo-Persian Oil Company, of the Suez Canal Company and the Eastern Telegraph Company; controlled the largest British domestic coal distributors, Wm Cory and Sons, was director of shipyards and steel works in Scotland, tea plantations, collieries, and so on. Shipping companies did not disclose their profits[17] — but the *Economist* of 18 July 1925 reported that an analysis of P&O's combined balance sheets during the previous quarter showed that, after paying debenture interest, the profits were £5,984,577, or an increase over 1924 of £795,879.[18] In 1924 P&O paid dividends of 12–15 per cent.

The Money Crisis in Britain

Despite the high dividends paid, British firms faced a serious problem in 1925. The economic slump affected every enterprise, and when trade declined, the shipping firms were bound to be hit. The crisis became particularly severe when the New York Federal Reserve Bank raised its discount rate from 3 to 3.5 per cent. To stop a flow of money to the US the British rate was raised on 5 March, from four per cent to five. This placed British exports at a disadvantage on the world market and the government had to choose between supporting industry or preserving Britain's position as the world's financial centre. Winston Churchill, the Chancellor of the Exchequer, was advised that it was the City (rather than industry) that had to be bolstered and he put England back on the gold standard, with the pound fixed at close to its pre-war value of $4.79 from the end of April 1925.

This was a gross over-valuation of the currency by approximately 10 per cent, and brought Britain to the brink of an economic crisis. British goods were now so overpriced on the world markets that trade dropped catastrophically. Consequently the employers decided to cut costs by 10 per cent starting with wages. The first industry in which this was attempted was coal mining, and this led to the confrontation on 31 July 1925, when the government was forced to retreat. The shipowners, in committee[19], also targeted transport workers. It was this that led directly to a wage cut from 1 August 1925, the very day after other unionists were shouting 'Victory'.

Such was the economic background to the events that led to the cut in the seamen's wages. It is doubtful whether they realised the nature of the problems that led to the reduction in their wages. What they did see was the effect of the cut on their slim resources. They came out on strike and many were to learn, from their own experiences and from the many statements they heard or read, the larger ramifications of the action they had taken. They took on forces that proved beyond their power to overcome:the employers, state power, and their own (official) trade union.

2

THE SEAFARERS AND THEIR ORGANIZATION

Put the Pound in the Plate!

On Sunday 28 June 1925, a special conference of the National Sailors and Firemen's Union of Great Britain and Ireland (NSFU) was convened. The delegates appeared to consist entirely of union officials and there is no indication that the membership was informed of, or aware of, its taking place. Yet, the purpose of the conference was to consider a proposal by Havelock Wilson that the Union offer the shipowners a reduction of wages.[1]

Wilson's address to the conference is informative, both for its style and for its contents. After a roll call of delegates he said:

> Well, gentlemen, I have no doubt that many of you when you got the circular convening this meeting were asking each other the question, 'I wonder what this is about'. On the other hand, I have no doubt that many of you had a shrewd idea what it was for. The real object of the meeting is to consider the serious state of affairs which exists in the shipping industry, not only in this country but in every maritime country in the world. I have been informed that the owners are seeking for some relief with regard to wages, and I have an idea that there are some owners who would like a cut of £3 per month, because they contend they are unable to run their ships on the freights that are current today.

Wilson then referred to a document on the wages paid to seamen in Europe, circulated to delegates. There it was claimed that most received less than half that paid by British shippers.

> What I want you to do, if my advice is worth having — and I suppose I am the President of this union because my advice is worth a little consideration — (hear, hear) — I want you to be wise, and if there is going to be a cut your duty to the men is to make that cut as small as you possibly can. (Hear, hear). The man who takes up that attitude is a wise man; he is a statesman . . .

To counter any possibility of delegates calling for a strike, he said there would be scabs who would gladly take the jobs in the event of such action. Among these he listed Arabs, non-union men and those who had been compelled to join the NSFU to secure a berth. He continued:

> Now we have got to watch and see that whatever cut is made is a small one. I always believe in the bold course. The general who knows when to rush in with a chance of success is generally the man who comes out on top. I can well

imagine that if in the ranks of the shipowners someone were to start about a cut of £3 a month, there would be any number who would join in that talk. My object is to prevent that from taking place, and so far I think I have been successful. I have heard rumours for a long time now; I have said nothing publicly because the least said sometimes the sooner it is mended. But when we get up to closer quarters − I spoke to many who I knew were holding responsible positions, and knowing that the wages question was to be discussed I begged of them that whatever discussion on wages was to take place they would not fix any demand. Do you see what I mean? − that they would not, for instance, send us along a notice to say that they wanted a reduction of £3 a month or any other sum; but rather that they would meet us to discuss the serious condition of the shipping trade and see whether any relief could be afforded.

Wilson continued, seemingly taking the audience into his confidence, but without producing any documents, or providing any hard information. He was offering them a ring-side seat where they could watch (approvingly!) but without really intervening. He continued:

I had an idea in my mind in doing that; because if we met the owners and there was any demand made [by them] for any particular sum, and we played the right part, I feel sure we would bring over from the owners' side a considerable amount of support; whereas, if a fixed sum were talked of, they would be like we are ... [that is, obdurate].

Now, I am going to advise you when we meet the owners that we should offer them to take off the £1 that we got last year. Everyone says we stole it. I believe that. We did ...[2]

Delegates were then invited to speak and most rose to support Wilson in his claims. Some underlined the dangers of strike action, saying there were over 5,000 men idle in Liverpool alone who would gladly scab if there was a strike. There was also praise for Wilson, and praise (from delegate Matt Tearle) for union policy:

There is no other Trade Union in Great Britain that has worked so harmoniously as we have worked with the shipowners, and when I say the shipowners I mean the National Maritime Board. That Board has shipowners represented on it.

However, any man who rose to question what was said, and there were a few, was ignored or quickly silenced, and some were told that their complaints had already been attended to. Wilson spoke paternalistically to the delegates saying that when he travelled on a ship and spotted faults, he had them rectified by talking to the owners. 'I venture to say', he told one delegate, 'that in a very short time some of the things that I found out will be adjusted. No one knows anything about that, but it is going on all the time'.

There was apparently no more to be said. Conference adopted a resolution instructing delegates to the Maritime Board to offer a £1 cut in wages. This it was stated would check demands by the shipowners for a higher reduction.

In some respects this tallies with the minutes of discussions at meetings of the Shipowners section of the National Maritime Board (NMB) and at the Shipping

Federation's Executive Council; but some discrepancies indicate that not all the facts were placed before the seamen's conference.[3]

Firstly, the situation leading up to the one pound increase in 1924 was not seen in quite the same way by the shipowners as Wilson had reported. The latter did not consider that the money had been 'stolen' but indeed thought that Wilson's demand was 'rather modest'. F C Allen reported that, with Cuthbert Laws, he met Wilson at the Shipowner's Section of the NMB in 1924. He continued:

> In my own humble view he wants £1. I think he was rather modest, in so much as he could well have asked us for two [pounds] and expected to get one, or something of that sort. But anyhow what he said was: 'We do not want any beating about the bush; we do not want to have any auctioning of this, but One Pound is the least I can talk of' — he must have £1 (*sic*).

Allen and Laws met with Wilson again and said there was no economic justification for an increase. However, said Allen:

> He recognized all that, but he says he is being pushed by the people below him and if a settlement is not come to there will be a row, and he implies that Cotter [of the Amalgamated Marine Workers Union] may go round the country and stir it up, and he is very anxious therefore to get a settlement as soon as he possibly can . . .

Wilson phoned Allen shortly thereafter to say that he had been criticized for not demanding more, and 'went through a very unpleasant afternoon'. It had therefore been agreed that the extra pound would be paid in two instalments and all that was in dispute was when the first 10s should be paid. The two part payments were made in June and September, restoring the position as of April 1923 and, although some shipowners grumbled, as indeed they would, the employers got off very lightly.

The second difference arose from a failure to disclose that the letter from the shipowners to the union only asked for the annulment of the increase of 1924 — with no demand for a higher deduction.[4] The Shipping Federation's position was outlined at a meeting of the Executive Council of 22 May 1925. Mr Dalgleish, moving the resolution on wage reduction, said that monthly wages paid on ships in Europe were far below British levels. That is: Spain £5 4s.6d, Germany £418s, and Italy (wages and provisions) £8 6s. Therefore, he said,

> . . . the time has arrived when the advance of wages granted to the transport workers and to all seafarers in 1924 should be withdrawn and notice be given immediately to the unions.

This was in line with the Ulster District Committee resolution:

> That in view of the continued and increasing depression in Shipping, both Deep-Sea and Coastwise Trades being equally affected, and also taking into consideration the lately revised scale of wages on German ships operative as from 1st April 1925, as compared with British vessels, this Committee recommends that the question of the necessity of a reduction in seamen's wages be brought before the Executive of the Shipping Federation, Ltd, at the earliest opportunity.

The Ulster committee claimed that shipping, particularly of coal, had declined sharply and that the lost volume could not be regained without drastic reductions in costs: that is by reducing dockers' wages and cutting the cost of trimming, loading, loading and discharging, piloting, and internal transport. This was a comprehensive list, and the Shipping Federation endorsed the demands which were aimed at every operation contributing to the cost of shipping. Obviously, they concluded, the 1924 wage increase to seafarers had to be revoked. A copy of the resolution was to be sent to Wilson and to Transport Workers officials, pilotage authorities, etc.

The base was laid for the meeting of the NMB at which Wilson could offer the shipowners a cut of one pound from 1 August 1925. That gathering, held on 3 July, was even more remarkable than those that preceded it. According to the published minutes of the NMB, Sir Frederick Shadworth Watts opened the meeting with a statement that the shipping trade was in bad shape, and called on the seamen to propose a reduction. Havelock Wilson rose in response and called for an amicable agreement:

> As you have so wisely said, perhaps [the shipping trade] has never been so bad as it is today . . . We do not want any argument just for the sake of 'manoeuvring for position', as they call it. Let us have none of that game! Let us be straight and plain!

Wilson then said that a conference had been called, and it had cost the union nearly £1,000 — indicating that it was in earnest in their intentions 'and were desirous of helping you [the shipowners] in every possible way':

> Now we come this morning, and we are going to say to you: 'Last year you were good enough to give us an advance of £1 a month' . . . Now we come, and having taken into consideration what you did last year, we have come to say this morning: 'We will give up that £1 at once' — without any argument, without any alarming statements about what is going to happen and so on. We do that, and I hope Mr Chairman, and you Gentlemen, will recognize that in doing that we are doing a manly thing, and certainly in the right spirit too — quite the right spirit. You might have come here and talk about 30s, or some other figure, but it is better for us to suggest the reduction, and when I say that is what we suggest I want you to understand that this is our offer, and we advise you strongly to accept it.

Wilson, undoubtedly referring to the threat of a general strike, warned of unrest in the country, and the importance of reaching a settlement in the same spirit as in the past. Then he spoke of the difficulties faced by shippers who ran their ships at a loss, many driven to the bankruptcy courts — 'So we offer you that £1'. He also felt obliged to appeal to the shipowners for sympathy — because his union officials would have 'to face the ordinary sailors, firemen, cooks and stewards' and he knew what they would have to go through:

> So far as I am concerned, there will be abuse heaped on me in tons. I do not hear it. I am not there. I am safely fixed in a place called St George's Hall. What does it matter to me if a fellow on a ship is cursing me and saying I ought to be shot? I do not hear it, and if anyone comes and tells me he has

been on a ship where they give me a very 'good' character, I am not concerned, because I do not hear it myself. But I know what my colleagues have to go through, and here is the remarkable part of the whole thing to me. The abuse which these good gentlemen will be subject to will not come from Union men, but from a lot of dirty useless rubbish. Somehow or other these fellows get on the ships, and they want to use the Union for their own purposes ...

Wilson inveighed against those who would not join the NSFU, or (foreseeing the consequences of the day's work) would not accept the wage reduction. He described such men as 'the biggest lot of blackguards I ever met in my life ... if I were a shipowner, I would be ashamed to carry them'. After assuring the employers that the reduction covered everyone (masters and officers excepted) who had benefited from the increase of 1924, it was only left for the meeting to agree that the reductions would take place from 1 August 1925.

The agreement was celebrated at a dinner at the Hotel Cecil on Thursday 23 July. A description of the event that appeared in the shipowner's journal *Fairplay* of 30 July said:

Some 400 guests, including well known shipowners and labour leaders and officials and many sailors, firemen and stewards with their wives sat down to dinner at the joint invitation of the Shipping Federation and the National Sailors' and Firemen's Union.

Toasts were proffered: to the seamen by Sir Alan Anderson (who presided) and to the shipowners, by Wilson, who reportedly said that in earlier fights, especially in those resulting from the Shipping Federation being formed: 'that the Shipowners were justified in what they did, and that he was wrong'. He was loudly applauded. The extent of the applause to this acceptance of strike breaking was not recorded: but seemingly, it was not altogether lost amidst the popping of champagne corks.

First Steps in Organizing the Firemen and Seamen[5]

The events of June and July 1925 were not exceptional inside the shipping trade. Shipowners and union officials would meet regularly, both formally and informally and, with a word here and a nod and a wink there, matters affecting the lives of 140,000 men were settled. This had become the practice only after 1911, when shippers and the seamen's union had found it more conducive to collaborate than to fight, but it had not always been the case.

The National Amalgamated Sailors' and Firemen's Union (later renamed the NSFU) was launched by J Havelock Wilson in 1887,[6] but met bitter opposition from the shipowners until 1911, when the NASFU was accorded recognition — although amicability was still some years away. Part of the problem faced by the union arose from the terms of association of the Shipping Federation Ltd, founded in 1890. 'From the first', says L H Powell, its official historian, 'the Federation was founded as a fighting machine to counter the strike weapon, and it made no secret of the fact'. The employers used 'depot ships', manned by potential scabs, to take over the running of strike-bound vessels and intended initially to control the labour force and break the union[7] The employers also insisted that seamen seeking a berth first obtain a 'Federation ticket', pledging the holder to serve alongside non-union seamen. This served a double purpose: it gave the employers a monopoly on labour recruitment and it blocked a 'closed shop'.

Conditions for organizing seamen worsened during the first decade of the 20th century, not only in Britain, but throughout Europe. Strike breakers were sent from Britain to Germany and Sweden in 1907/8. In 1909 the shipowners were united in an International Shipping Federation. The International Transport Workers' Federation (ITWF), to which the NSFU was initially affiliated, seemed to be the last bastion against the attacks of the employers, but it had few resources and was ineffectual.

It was at this juncture that a strike was planned, to take effect at the end of 1910 or early 1911. The ITWF urged caution, believing that a strike could not succeed and the large European unions withdrew support. Only the Belgian and Dutch sections supported the strike when it commenced on 14 June 1911 in Britain. Ironically, the newly founded National Transport Workers' Federation in Britain, which was expected to join the strike, withdrew at the last minute. Yet despite the pessimistic forecasts of the two federal bodies, the time was propitious for strike action. Shipping activity in 1911 was at an all-time high, trade was booming, and freight rates were high. There was little unemployment and there were few scabs available in the event of a strike.

The NSFU called the seamen out and the men won a resounding victory. The union was recognized in many ports and the seamen won wage increases.[8] The factors leading to success differed from port to port. In Southampton the men struck five days early and the employers conceded defeat before other ports came out. This bolstered other strikers, leading to concessions, albeit after violence (and some casualties) in Hull, Glasgow, and elsewhere.[9] The seamen's action also dovetailed with that of dockers and this strengthened both groups of workers.[10] But the most important factor was the mobilization of the seamen. In this Wilson was fortunate in having the backing of Tom Mann, just returned from Australia, and of Joe Cotter and Frank Pearce of the ship's stewards.

Cotter, Pearce and Mann, who played different parts in the strike, were syndicalists — although there is little evidence that this philosophy had any impact on the seamen. Mann was involved in all the transport strikes of the year — some of which overlapped the seamen's strike, and others following an independent course; Cotter's and Pearce's intervention brought the stewards and cooks into the strike.[11] In Cardiff it was Wilson's crony, 'Captain' Edward Tupper, who played a major role in bringing out the seamen.[12]

The strike of 1911 was a high point in the seamen's union militancy and took place at a time of intensified trade union struggle throughout the country.[13] It marked the beginning of recognition for the seamen's union, although it was another two years before a national wage increase was granted and the closed shop and negotiating machinery were instituted.[14]

Recognition and a Split

Following the strike of 1911, Wilson invited any three shipowners to visit the NSFU offices and inspect its books and documents. It is not known whether any inspection followed, but some of the employers were impressed and thereafter there was some co-operation between the two sides. However the Shipping Federation still remained implacably opposed to any unionization.

The strike of 1911 split the union apart — and this was to become a factor in the events of 1925. There are two (possibly complementary) reasons to explain what happened. According to Mogridge, a large number of members were enrolled in Southampton, where the strike was settled first, and the branch soon accumulated £1,000. Union officials demanded the money under the rules of the NSFU,[15] but the branch balked, and demanded a full inquiry into the financial control and management of the union before making any payment. When Wilson rejected their demand the branch broke away. However according to Shinwell the Southampton branch defected because Wilson accepted a smaller wage increase than was promised, on the understanding with the shippers that employment would be made available only to men who joined the NSFU.[16]

In August 1912 the Glasgow branch seceded and joined the Southampton men to form the British Seafarers Union (BSU). Here too there are two versions of events. Mogridge says that Shinwell (seconded to assist in the organization of Clydeside seamen) recruited shore-workers who prepared the ships for putting out to sea — considering them valuable allies in any future dispute. This was countermanded by Wilson and he also had the committee officials in Glasgow dismissed. This led to the secession of the entire branch. Shinwell says only that dockers, who were unorganized at the time, had come out in sympathy with the seamen, and had responded to meetings he addressed. The break, according to Shinwell was occasioned by Wilson 'closing the branch because we had obtained the higher rate of pay'. It has not been possible to check these different stories but, whatever the cause, the unions broke apart.

The War and a National Wage Agreement

When war came, seamen were affected by the wave of patriotism that swept all Britain and their ability to keep open the lines of communication and supplies won them fervent support. The men of the merchant marine were regaled for their heroism — the shipowners, with somewhat less publicity, reaped the profits of war. Many of these facts lay concealed during the long years of war but details were widely broadcast during the strike of 1925, when radical papers printed accounts of profits and losses.

The war also affected the working of the unions. Their leaders became Empire loyalists and active recruiters for the war effort. Shinwell claims that he undertook 'certain duties on behalf of both the Admiralty and the newly created Ministry of Shipping' and this included collecting reluctant crews and prevailing on them to 'accept employment on auxiliary vessels'.[17]

The seamen kept the sea lanes open, and many lost their lives with union leaders acting as cheer-leaders. Havelock Wilson, according to Mogridge, threw 'himself into the war against Germany with all the fierce energy and virulent oratory that had previously been directed against the [Shipping] Federation'. Furthermore, he 'stumped the country making jingoistic speeches' and dispatched 'Captain' Tupper 'to break up meetings of pacifists'. The devastating effect of U–Boat action, and in particular the sinking of the *Lusitania*, with the loss of more than 1,000 lives, made Wilson's task comparatively easy. In the process he became an establishment figure, viciously anti-Labour, anti-German, and (after 1917) anti-Bolshevik. His patriotism and his war-time services earned him the CBE.

The seamen did not share this enthusiasm. There was growing resentment over wages and working conditions, and anger over the prosecutions of men who were accused of desertion when they transferred to the US navy (which paid higher war-rates). Meanwhile the war brought the NSFU and the Shipping Federation closer together. Spurred on by the new identity of interests a number of issues were agreed. There was a substantial pay rise, a national wage agreement was negotiated and joint control in recruiting crews was established. Finally, in November 1917, the National Maritime Board (NMB) was formed, composed of members of the Shipping Federation and the NSFU, and chaired by a civil servant from the Ministry of Shipping. This body effectively took over the regulation of the war-time agreements, and also acted as the arbitration board for the industry. In 1919 the NMB was made a permanent institution, but without the member from the Ministry.

The new arrangement did not go unchallenged. Vigilance Committees were formed in Liverpool, with nuclei in Glasgow and London'[18] who opposed the collaboration with the shipowners. and to Wilson's autocratic treatment of all opposition.The resentment grew in May 1921 when wages were cut by £2 10s. When the Committees tried to have the wage cut reversed Wilson met their challenge by changing the NSFU's voting regulations, denying them the possibility of obtaining office.[19]

The Amalgamated Marine Workers Union

In the years to come all arrangements in the merchant marine were finalized by the NMB, with the NSFU claiming the right to act for all seamen in Great Britain and Ireland. Besides small associations serving specialist interests (like the telegraphists) there were two effective organizations outside the NSFU – the BSU and the Cooks and Stewards' Union, led by Joe Cotter.The latter union broke with Wilson when he agreed to an all-round wage cut in 1921 and, when they called a strike for its restoration, officials of the NSFU obtained scabs for the employers.[20] The strike collapsed and more than 17,000 men left the Cooks and Stewards Union, forcing them to seek an alliance with some other body. The BSU, confined to Glasgow, Southampton and London, also sought allies and, on the initiative of the National Transport

Workers' Federation, the two unions combined in the Amalgamated Marine Workers' Union (AMWU) on 1 January 1922.[21]

In a move designed to counter the AMWU and stop the development of a potentially more militant union, the Port Consultant's Card, or PC5, was introduced in April 1922 in collusion with Wilson. Seamen in search of a berth were required to produce the card, duly stamped by the NSFU to show that membership was in good standing, and counter-stamped by the employers. The PC5, which became a bone of contention between the NSFU and its rival unions, was used by the former as an inducement for men to pay their subscriptions. At a meeting of the executive of the union on 23 April 1922, an official named Bond was minuted as saying:

> The first day they had it in operation was on Friday, and they would be amazed to realize the change it had brought about. *Men who, for various reasons, because they had not paid up perhaps for a long period, came cap in hand to try and get the PC5 card* ... [T]he results already obtained had been most satisfactory ... on Saturday alone, a day when usually they could not collect a tanner, they had obtained the sum of £60 from the men signing on. He was glad of the arrangement, because it had established a better spirit with the [Shipping] Federation Offices ...[22]

Union officials became increasingly arrogant and, according to Lindop, they would beat up men who would not take the PC5. The AMWU was badly affected, although initially it claimed that exclusion from the agreement was a good thing. Thus Joseph Cotter, the President, said on 9 January 1922:

> ... the new union was not attached to the National Maritime Board, and apologized to no one because of it. They were going to have no faking at all. They were not going to have any Shipping Masters interfering with the union ...[23]

However, the NSFU and the NMB used the card to prevent other bodies taking part in any negotiations. The AMWU lost members and in 1922 published a pamphlet against the PC5 Card claiming that the NSFU regarded seafarers as:

> ... chattels to be handled about by the officials of the Sailors' and Firemen's Union and the Shipping Federation; neither your bodies nor your souls belong to yourselves. As a matter of fact, if this gang had their way you would be in the position of the chattel slaves of a hundred years ago.

Finally, in May 1923 Shinwell raised the matter of the PC5 in Parliament and asked the representative of the Board of Trade to institute an enquiry into the method of engaging seamen. The following day Shinwell told the Congress of the Seamen's Section of the ITWF that:

> After I had stated my case, there arose from the Government benches a shipowner, who is a member of the Shipping Federation, and who employs a great deal of Chinese labour. He claimed that the shipowners were entitled to make the arrangements they had with the [NSFU] because the body does everything the shipowners asks them to do.[24]

There was little the AMWU could do and it was powerless when the NSFU agreed to wage cuts. Only on one occasion did its members take strike action. In

April 1923 some 200 firemen in Southampton came out with their union's backing, and were joined by some members of the NSFU on unofficial strike. However, the action was limited and scabs were easily found. The strike collapsed and 134 men were arrested for breaking their articles.[25]

Although there were ports where it was not essential to carry the Card to get a berth, many seamen had to join the NSFU to get a job. Despite this, militant seamen with pre-war syndicalist ideas were vigorously opposed to any institutions in which the employers were involved. The AMWU pamphlet claimed that at a union meeting convened to discuss the card it was said that:

> ... a lot of fellows hate the sight of the Shipping Federation and say they would not be found lying dead in the company of a Shipping Federation official ... They suggest that after having fought the Federation they are being driven back to them.

The TUC intervened in March 1924 when it tried to bring the two unions together. However the discussions broke down over Wilson's demands that the joint body be subordinatedto himself and the NSFU officials. Thos was obviously unacceptable to the leaders of the AMWU and the talks were abandoned.

The problem lay not only in the attitude taken by Wilson and the NSFU: all was not well inside the AMWU. There was simmering discontent for some time and this surfaced on 23 March 1925, when five officials, consisting of former members of the BSU were dismissed by a majority vote and Cotter and Shinwell hurled abuse at each other.[26] The internal squabbling continued and intensified — and Cotter's supporters claimed that the AMWU was in deep decline and should be disbanded. Cotter, despairing of any progress, was obviously in contact with Wilson and the NSFU and preparing to change allegiance.[27]

On 4 April, at an Executive Council meeting, the AMWU was said to have total assets of £27,773, with nine branches in Britain and one at Antwerp. However the Glasgow branch was inactive and the Liverpool delegate, fearing that more money might be squandered over and above the £100,000 which he claimed had been used without any benefit to the seamen, called for dissolution.

Then at the annual conference Cotter, the president, claimed that the AMWU had almost ceased to exist and that there were no more than 1,800 members throughout the country. This was the prelude to a turbulent meeting. Cotter was called upon to resign, to pay rent for the union house he occupied and to sign the union cheques which he steadfastly refused to do. Cotter's friends were accused of sabotaging efforts to build branches and even the majority who wanted to build the AMWU could bring little news of success. Yet, three facts emerged at the conference that were to have a bearing on coming events. Firstly it was announced that the Southampton branch was making progress and was committed to the union and secondly, that Shinwell had come to an agreement with some tug, hopper and dredger firms that only AMWU men would be employed. As Warner, the London delegate reported: 'It was, really speaking, a PC5 of our own'(!)

The third item came from Shinwell and carried a message that at that stage was not altogether clear. Almost casually, he informed the conference delegates:

I am just going to tell you something ... that I have got from the NSFU officials themselves, they told me they expected to be up against something, so
we must prepare when that something happens, and be assured we will be
prepared, and take advantage of it (loud cheers).

This was the first public intimation of the events that were to lead up to the
seamen's strike. Yet despite this knowledge nothing was done to pursue the matter
further or to take the initiative in preparing for 'that something' which was about to
happen. The leaders of the AMWU knew how to exchange insults with the NSFU,
but they did not have the heart to prepare for action against the shipowners.

Control of the Seamen's Union

The National Maritime Board was the conciliation body in the world of the
mercantile marine. It was here that shipowners met with the leaders of the
NSFU, and in the words of Sir Walter Runciman '[sat] in Conference together, and discuss in harmony the small and big things that surround their
respective avocations'.[28]

There was more praise for Havelock Wilson in Powell's official history of the
Shipping Federation. In a brief entry on page 127 he said:

These pages have been peppered with the name of Mr Havelock Wilson. He
was a maker of industrial history and a product of his times. The collective
feelings of shipowners towards him changed in 30 years from something
perilously near hatred to genuine admiration. No trade union leader of his
generation made a more lasting impression on his time. He was fearless and
far-sighted. And once he had become convinced of the need for collective
bargaining, for honouring agreements and for industrial peace, he fought for
all these with all his unsurpassed tenacity.

However, outside the statements made by his friends among the shipowners,
the comments on the career of Wilson become less complimentary and more acer-
bic. G D H Cole and Raymond Postgate, after saying that in his early years Wilson
did 'good work' for the seamen, then added on page 435 that: 'before long [he] had
acquired for himself a more disagreeable reputation than any contemporary
British trade union leader'.

Alan Bullock the historian was more damning. He said that the NSFU was

... under the despotic control of Havelock Wilson, [it] had become a company union working hand in glove with the employers in the Shipping
Federation. Membership was enforced by the employers and in return Wilson ruthlessly suppressed any demand — the eight hour day, for instance —
which might inconvenience the shipowners. Little was done for the seamen,
whose conditions were amongst the worst in any industry. Yet so complete
was the hold which Wilson and the shipowners together exercised over the
engagement of seamen that it was difficult to remedy what had become an
open scandal. Any protest, leave alone attempts to start a rival union, was
certain to be followed by the dismissal and victimization of the men involved.[29]

It was left to those who confronted him in action to produce the more damaging details. William Gallagher, Clydeside rebel and later member of the CPGB, after referring to Wilson's sabotaging of the Stockholm peace conference in 1917, described one incident in his memoir on pages 187–8:

Havelock Wilson ... the greatest patriot of all the trade union leaders, fresh from his victory in getting the sailors to refuse to sail the ship in which Macdonald was booked to travel to the Stockholm conference, came to Glasgow about this time for a great jingo meeting ...

Entrance was by ticket only, but radicals printed copies and distributed them to oppositionists ...

But Wilson wasn't depending on tickets alone to secure a meeting. He brought a crowd of gangsters from the north of England to St Andrew's Hall and served them out with a considerable supply of booze. It was one of the earliest applications of fascist methods in the country, with a guaranteed police protection.

Yet these brief and anecdotal accounts do not allow the reader to see the man behind the screen that he seems to have so carefully erected. Most of what is known about Havelock Wilson was filtered through his own hands. He was always anti–socialist and never joined the parliamentary Labour Party, although he sat in the house as a Liberal almost continuously after 1892. He differed from other trade unionists, he said in his autobiography,

... on the question of the destruction of the so-called capitalist system. My theory is, right or wrong, I want every man to be a capitalist, because as long as a man has money and he is taken away from the poverty line he becomes an independent and free man ... (p 187).

Whether Wilson 'had money' is not known, but he certainly lived well above the poverty line. In 1921 he received from the NSFU £1,000 per year plus expenses, a motor car and chauffeur and a private residence at the union's headquarters for himself and his wife. In addition he earned £400 a year as an MP.[30] This was a handsome salary in those years. Wilson undoubtedly funded the movements he sponsored over the years and he was not short of financial resources.

On 9 October 1925, during the strike, the *Westralian Worker* printed extracts from a book by Frank Anstey, an Australian Labour MP, entitled *Red Europe*.

In the House of Commons, Mr Pringle, Liberal MP said the English institution for the corruption of men and women was started as a section of the Ministry of Munitions under Lloyd George, and was afterwards linked to the Ministry of Information. He stated that large pecuniary inducements were held out to trade union officials — and sometimes with success — to make secret reports as to 'agitators' and 'anti–patriots' inside the unions. Havelock Wilson of the Seamen's Union, was openly charged by Arthur Henderson with handling £50,000 of which he, Wilson, dared not explain the origin. Tom Richardson, MP alleged that clerical work for Wilson's Patriotic Crusade was done in the war office. 400 Patriotic Trade Unionists, at £1 per day and expenses, were engaged to demonstrate in Coventry against the munition strikers.

Wilson's jingoism was followed by an unscrupulous appeal to Hugo Stinnes, the armaments manufacturer, in early 1922 for money.[31] This, together with his strike breaking activities during the war, and his launching of the 'Industrial Peace Union of the British Empire' in October 1926 indicates a likeness to the labour leaders who later collaborated with the fascists of Mussolini's Italy. The advertisement sponsoring the Industrial Peace Union said:

Give the Old Country a Chance
It is a Workers' Movement, an Employers'
Movement and a Patriotic Movement.
Five Years of Industrial Peace will
Save the Country and the Empire.
Do your Bit, Workers, Employers and all
grades of Society. Join up with the
Forces of INDUSTRIAL PEACE
and help defeat the Reds.[32]

Officials of the union were men hand-picked by Wilson. They were all full time officials, and none went to sea. In fact, many had never been to sea at all — and among the most notorious was 'Captain' Edward Tupper, 'VC'. Tupper's VC was as spurious as his captaincy and almost the only thing about him that was not in doubt was his inability to tell the truth. He also had a propensity for violence and an undoubted talent for raising scabs to break the 1925 strike.

Our knowledge of much of Tupper's activities comes from his autobiography and if the facts must remain in doubt (because of the strange mix of fantasy and fact in whatever he said), his intentions are clear. In chapter four we note his claims that in 1911 he organized race riots in Cardiff, where he had been sent by Wilson to organize the strike. His boasts were that in 1925 he established close co-operation with the Shipping Federation when he took over control of the NSFU while Wilson and Cotter were on their Canadian cruise (see chapter nine)that he had worked with the shipowners to lessen the impact of the strike in Australia (p 276), and arranged for the deployment of scabs in Britain (p 274).

The seamen's monthly shillings were used to provide the funds for hiring strong-arm men, for raising and transporting scabs during strikes and for the many projects including the 'Industrial Peace Union' designed to fight the 'reds'. Yet it seems that the NSFU provided no funds for the welfare of its members. It certainly made no contributions 'for sickness, idleness or striking'.[33]

The Voice of the Seamen

Little of the seamen's disaffection with the shipowners and the union has been recorded, and much of the information about the (presumably vocal) Liverpool Vigilance Committee has come mainly from Wilson's letter in 1926 (see above). The position of workers in the union in the 1920s was one of subordination. Wilson and the officials entrenched themselves, negotiated with the employers and rarely (if ever) consulted the membership.

During the voyage the men were compartmentalized, deckhands generally mixing together and firemen and cooks forming their own special group. While some men managed to stay together on the same vessel over several years, others moved from ship to ship after spending a short time in port. There is no indication of any union activity in port or on board ship, and the union did not figure as part of the men's work experience. In a commentary, the *Glasgow Forward* said on 29 August 1925:

> Now, one readily admits that a Seamen's Union must of necessity have less of a democratic control than is customary in other unions. The ships come and go. Men cannot in the very nature of things attend branch meetings. It may even be the case that decisions must frequently be taken without it being possible to consult anything more than a fraction of the membership.
>
> But Mr Havelock Wilson's Union has long been notorious, or shall we say unique, in its methods . . .

Unique it was and when asked publicly (on board SS *Mauritania*, New York, 20 September 1925) why no ballot was taken when negotiations were opened on the reduction of wages, he said the union was 'not compelled, according to the rules, to take any such ballot'. A ballot was only required on a call to strike. However, as he had declared earlier in this address, the last strike he had called was in 1911 and he did not intend calling another, the conclusion was obvious.

The situation was altered only when the men were involved in a struggle and made public their dissatisfactions. Thus, on 2 October 1925, when interviewed by the *Westralian Worker*, a seaman replied to questions:

Q: Who are the officers of the Seamen's union [in London]?

A: This is a thing we are all asking. We do not know who the officers are; meetings of the union are never called; matters of great importance to the workers employed on board ship are never discussed. As a matter of fact all we know about our union is that Havelock Wilson is the president, and that some representative of it must give us a PC5 before we can get a job. We can tell you all about the conditions on the vessels, all about the work we do; but don't ask us anything about our union affairs because we don't know; we never hear of them.

Q: But you elect your officials annually, don't you?

A: Elect officers? No, the officers of the British Seamen's Union are not elected annually or otherwise. I have been a member of the British Seamen's Union for years and I have never been asked to vote on anything . . . Although we are fully paid–up members of the union we know nothing whatever about its affairs the only thing we are allowed to know is when there is a reduction in wages . . . Then we get a radio message from Havelock Wilson telling us what to do.

And what they were to do was obvious. They had to accept the position and go about their work.

3

THE STRIKE BEGINS IN BRITAIN

Prelude to the General Strike

It is arguable that the period 1910 to 1926 is the most bitter period of class warfare in modern British history. From 1922 onwards the workers were defeated and subdued in one industry after another. The General Strike was the majestic but pathetic epitaph to their struggle.

Gareth Steadman Jones[1]

In the several published accounts of the General Strike of 1926, few have considered that event as the culmination of a period of increasingly bitter class warfare and not one has mentioned the seamen's strike that commenced on 2 August 1925 and extended to October or later. Even at the time, only the *Marine Worker* editorial of September 1925, discussing the wage cut in the merchant marine, grasped the significance of Havelock Wilson's role.[2]

Since 30 June 1925 the attention of union leaders had been fixed on the threat to wage levels. The coal mine operators had given the statutory one months notice of termination of the 1921 national agreement with the Miners Federation of Great Britain. Thereafter the guaranteed minimum wage would be replaced by locally negotiated wages. This would lead to a drop of 10–25 per cent or more.[3] The Miner's Federation called on the Trades Union Congress (TUC) for assistance and, after talks between miners and mine owners collapsed, a national strike was planned. The miners needed the co-operation of all transport workers to stop the movement of coal supplies and for this the seamen would play a key role. The entire labour movement was mobilized during the month of July and a conference, attended by a thousand delegates, met on 31 July to pledge support in the struggle.

The government was determined to stop the unions but was not yet fully prepared. Since 1919–21 there had been draft plans to counter major industrial unrest but the machinery was dated and depended on the existence of a large army. This was discussed by the Cabinet in 1924 and although, according to the minutes, no emergency was anticipated at the time, the Home Secretary was authorized to renovate the plans. These were not yet complete in July 1925 – and it was feared that industrial paralysis would overtake the country before 'volunteers' could be mobilized.[4] The government's view was communicated to the King:

Many members of the Cabinet think that the struggle is inevitable and must come sooner or later: the P M does not share this view. The majority of the

Cabinet regard the present moment as badly chosen for the fight, though the conditions would be more favourable nine months hence . . .[5]

Consequently, the Cabinet decided to subsidize the coal mines to maintain the minimum wage for nine months while, ostensibly, an inquiry into the productive efficiency of the industry was conducted. This halted plans for strike action.

Leaders of the Labour Party were ecstatic. *Red Friday* (as 31 July was named) was described by the *Daily Herald* the following day, as 'the biggest victory the labour movement has won yet in the course of its history'. Communist Party writers were also exultant, although the party's paper warned in an editorial that this was 'an unstable peace' and would only lead 'to renewed class conflict'. The editor maintained that the loss of Britain's industrial monopoly necessitated a reduction of prices in foreign markets. This would drive the employers to reduce wages, although the return to gold had 'increased the value of the holdings of the rentiers in land industry and war loan stocks by about £1,000,000,000'. Indeed, it was said, there was a possibility that during this nine months' truce the 'capitalist class will launch an attack upon some other bodies of workers'.[6]

Yet, not a mention in this editorial of the cut in seamen's wages or of the strike that had already been declared in ports across the land. Instead the editorial looked inwards and directed attention to the coming Labour Party conference, restricting its demands to a call for an end to discrimination against communists, to allow affiliation of the CPGB to the Labour Party and to replace the existing reformism with 'a fighting workers' policy'.

The National Minority Movement

In November 1923, workers inside the miners, railwaymen and engineers' unions met with members of the CPGB and formed 'minority groups'. This was followed by a conference on 23 August 1924 to launch the National Minority Movement (NMM): 'to act as a point of crystallization' inside trade unions in Britain and 'to organize the working masses of Great Britain for the overthrow of capitalism'.[7] Initially the NMM aimed to strengthen workshop organization, create one union for each industry, enrol all workers in the unions, and defend wages against further cuts.

The NMM was affiliated with the Red International of Labour Unions (RILU or Profintern), which had its headquarters in Moscow. To further the aims of the RILU in Britain it was proposed that an Anglo-Russian trade union committee be established, and that through contact between leaders of the RILU and the TUC, there could be progress towards unity between the social democratic International Federation of Trade Unions and the Russian dominated RILU. This aim dominated NMM policies and was to determine events through 1925 and the general strike of 1926.

Sometime in 1924, George Hardy, one time leading member of the Industrial Workers of the World (IWW) who was in charge of the RILU seamen's section in Hamburg, returned to Britain. Elected national organizational secretary of the NMM, Hardy created a British seamen's section.[9] A small number of seamen in

London, belonging to either the NSFU or the AMWU, joined the seamen's section of the minority movement in mid–July 1924.[10] Its significance for the events that followed the wage cut was its presence in London. The unofficial strike committee that was set up in early August invited Hardy to join them and he devoted his time to the working of the strike committee. This gave the *Workers Weekly* (organ of the NMM and the RILU) direct access to the strikers.

RILU policy was laid down for Britain by its leading theoretician in Moscow, Lozovsky. He demanded protection for 'revolutionary trade unionists' from the reformist leadership, but, he warned, the unity of the trade unions had to be maintained: they had to be held together, unified, and captured for communism. In line with this policy the NMM repeatedly said it had no intention of splitting any trade union or of forming splinter unions. This policy, seemingly admirable in principle, was to the detriment of the seamen. Unable to unseat the leaders of the NSFU, or to convince other trade unions that their cause needed support, the seamen had nobody to present their case. In this case the only way forward was to break away from the union that claimed to speak in their name. By maintaining the unity of their official organization, the strikers ended by being split in their action.

The Move to Strike Action

During July attention was focused on events in the coal fields and little attention was given by the labour movement to press reports that the National Maritime Board intended cutting seamen's wages on 1 August. The seamen did not act to counter the move and the AMWU, despite being forewarned by Shinwell, remained dormant.

In mid-July the newly formed seamen's section of the NMM declared that it would fight against wage reductions and would demand that a special rank and file delegate conference be convened, with full powers to ratify or reject any agreements on wages and working conditions. The NMM also called for an eight hour day for all ratings and, highlighting pressing complaints, demanded beds, blankets and cooking utensils for all seamen.

There is no evidence to suggest that the any group had plans to call the seamen out when the cuts were implemented. The *Workers Weekly*, which appeared on Saturday 1 August, had an article by Hardy, mentioning the cut and calling for an alliance of miners, railwaymen, transport workers and engineers. He proposed a programme for the seamen that included a 10 per cent rise in wages and time and a half for overtime, an eight hour day for deckhands and six hours below, provision of bedding; new radical conditions for men leaving ships and returning home. He also called for the right to form ship's committees to represent the men in any complaints at sea and a closed shop. Hardy spoke of 'prepar[ing] to resist the reductions on 1 August' and, in a monumental miscalculation, said that the 25,000 registered unemployed would not scab, because 'they will realize that our fight is their fight'.

The only report of seamens' protest came from Hull on 31 July. The local branch of the AMWU, obviously ahead of the national body, convened a meeting that was attended by about 200 seamen. It was resolved that men would be urged not to accept a berth except at the old rate of pay and that they would insist on the abolition of the PC5. It was also announced that the action would be unofficial and that there would be no strike pay.[11] Yet, after the initial meeting, there seem to have been no stoppages in Hull.[12]

Reports on the seamen's action were confused by the bias of the reporters and the institutions they supported. R E Bond, who was associated with the NMM, claimed retrospectively that the strike in Britain commenced on 2 August 'when large numbers of seamen refused to sign articles in the London Docks'. Yet, if there were such men, their action was spontaneous and there was no organization to support them. Bond also stated that a strike committee was formed on the 8th of August.[13] Yet the *Workers Weekly* of 14 August which had two articles on seamen carried no news of seamen striking. It only reported on 21 August that a strike committee of six had been elected at a mass meeting of seamen in Canning Town and that arrangements had been made for picketing and for meetings, 'with the result that several ships were held up [in London], the men refusing to sign on'. Also on Sunday 16th about 2,500 seamen, firemen and supporters marched through the streets of Poplar (East End of London), behind a banner:[14]

SEAMEN AND FIREMEN ARE FIGHTING FOR BREAD FOR THE KIDDIES.

The existence of an unofficial strike was mentioned on the 18th in the *Daily Herald*. The only other news of strike action came from Newcastle, where seamen met and pledged themselves not to sign articles at the reduced rate of pay. At least two ships were delayed during the next few days, in each case because seamen demanded the old rate of pay.[15] At this juncture newspaper reports diverged even further in their coverage of events at the ports. The conservative press dismissed talk of stoppages, speaking only of short delays or of the strike collapsing. The labour and communist press mentioned strike action and picketing, although the action was limited to a few ports. For example, the clerical staff of the Dundalk and Newry Steam Packet Co in Liverpool walked out on the 19th over salary cuts. They were followed by the dockers and shipping services came to a halt.[16]

On 22 August it was reported that members of the NSFU and the AMWU were on the Central Strike Committee (CSC) in London assisted by members of the NMM. However, it seems more likely that it was the NMM that seized the advantage of launching the committee and that they controlled the CSC throughout the strike, their members being drawn mainly from the NSFU.

From the beginning the issue of scabbing had to be faced. Shipowners and officials of the NSFU worked together to break the strike and both recruited crews from among seafarers and, where necessary, from untrained men. But in many ports where unemployment among seamen was endemic, there was little problem in signing up a crew, albeit with a short delay. Men were also deterred at the docks by the announcement that there would be no strike pay, no unemployment dole, and no poor laws relief for men who did not accept berths.

To secure crews for strike-bound ships, the employers first mobilized men in London and arranged to have them bussed to the docks. They then brought in men from further afield. The strikers tried to reach the men to win their support and bus drivers, railwaymen and others, refused to carry scabs,[17] but it was always an unequal struggle. Subterfuge was also used by the employers to stop the men striking. One account that we received probably accounts for some of the ships that just kept sailing even at the height of the strike. T R Patten of Plymouth, in a letter to the authors, stated that he had been an assistant baker on the *Empress of France*. The ship came into Southampton from Canada in the summer of 1925, and after passengers for the UK had disembarked, the men who expected to go ashore found the gangway blocked by the Master-at-Arms and two of his staff. Notices were posted up cancelling shore leave and the puzzled men were told that there was free beer in the bonded store.

All the bar-keepers were busy opening bottles of beer, pouring the contents into enamel pails. It was a case of bring your own jug or container. I well recall a cook returning to the galley with a bucket full, and a baker with a gallon measure full.

This continued until 2.30 pm when news came through that an attempted strike had collapsed, and that men due for leave could go ashore. Patten concludes:

No doubt the support of the *E/France's* crew had been expected, the Company's officials knew of this hence the free beer when the crew were kept on board.

The press said nothing of this kind of incident. In a brief reference to the ships that had just sailed, the *Evening News* of 7 September said: 'The *Empress of France* too was able to depend on her old crew'.

It was not certain in the latter part of August that the strike would spread, and even the dispatch of representatives from the CSC in London, to ports around the country, seemed to have only limited effect, even if the *Daily Herald* of 22 August could report that 35 ships were held up in the Thames, 'between the Port of London and Gravesend'. Then came the news that the seamen who arrived in Australia on 20 August had resolved to walk out, followed a few days later by similar announcements from South Africa and New Zealand. The strike could be said to have taken root from that point onwards.

Two days later, on the 22nd, firemen walked off the *SS Orbita* in Southampton five minutes before it was due to depart for New York. But many rejoined the ship and extra men were brought in by tender, allowing the ship to sail. Other liners raised their gangways early to prevent similar walk-offs. There was news in the press of meetings, of the setting up of strike committees in many major ports, and reports of clashes with police and of further recruiting of scabs.[18]

Tension was building up and it was reported that some NSFU officials were carrying guns.[19] On Thursday 27 August, George Reed, the branch secretary in Stepney, for reasons that were never satisfactorily explained, fired four shots at a meeting of seamen from his room above the union office. Richard Cocklin, who tried to stop him, was shot and injured. Reed handed his revolver to a policeman and was reported as saying: 'Here you are. What would you do if you had Roumanian Jews coming over here and smashing up our homes'? He appeared in court and was given bail of £100, for which the General Secretary acted as surety. Reed was sent to the union's convalescent home. At trial, he was found not guilty of attempted murder. He claimed that he had fired over the heads of the crowd to disperse them and that he had only recently borrowed the gun from a colleague, because he had been threatened.[20] There the matter was allowed to rest.

By now officials of the union were actively engaged in recruiting scabs, and moved men from areas of high unemployment to ports where the strikers were active. Tupper boasted of 'fetch[ing] loyal union crews from all over the shop' and getting them aboard liners at night.[21] The shipowners were doing the same and during the dispute moved some 3,500 seamen from one district to another to make up crews and took steps to stop the activities of pickets.

The AMWU Backs the Strike

The strike spread to many ports and received extra impetus after news arrived that men had walked off the ships in South Africa and Australasia, but the main centre of action in Britain was Southampton, the point of departure for southern seas. On 30 August a mass meeting in Southampton was addressed by Cannon, Shinwell, and McKinley, president, organizer and general secretary, respectively, of the AMWU. The seamen, many of whom were members of the NSFU, gave unanimous support for strike action against the wage cut, and protested against the stopping of allotment pay to families of the men who had taken action abroad. A strike committee was formed (presumably independent of the London committee) and the men resolved to approach other seamen to join them in strike action. Cables were sent to Australia and South Africa congratulating the men on their 'gallant stand' against the wage cut.[22]

The intervention of the AMWU was crucial. In Britain it came when the strike was faltering and for many strikers abroad the AMWU became the centre through which they could present their demands.[23] Yet there was no satisfactory reason for the long delay in swinging behind the strike. Nor was any reason given for the AMWU's failure to call out its members on the tugs.[24] Without the tugs, as is discussed below, the ships could not have left port, yet despite protests from the NMM and the London strikle committee, they continued to work throughout the strike.

Shinwell was silent on the issue of the tugs and he gave several explanations for the delay in coming to the support of the strike . He was reported by the *Daily Record and Mail* as saying firstly (on 1 September) that the AMWU had no alternative but to intervene because the seamen had never been consulted over the wage cut, and because of the decision to prosecute seamen who were on strike abroad. Then, according to the issue of 3 September, he told a meeting of 4,000 seamen in Liverpool about a 'conspiracy' between Havelock Wilson and Joseph Cotter, holding up union funds, work and activities for a period of five months which extended well into August.[25]

By 15 September Shinwell produced a third version of the AMWU's tardiness in joining the strike. His statement, reprinted in the *Forward* of 19 September, said:

The Marine Workers' Union was reluctant to enter another struggle, because on the last occasion when a wage revision took place their men were blacklegged by men belonging to Havelock Wilson's Union, and the [AMWU] suffered considerably as a result.

But the fight was forced upon us, and we had our members solidly behind us in declining to depart from the mandate that had been given us which was to fight all wage reductions.

Cannon, president of the AMWU, presented the case somewhat differently. In the *Southern Daily Echo* of 2 September he declared:

There is no 'Red' plot. It is a bread and butter plot. Ever since August 1st seamen and firemen of Southampton have been chafing under the reduction of wages. They know that the miners were successful in resisting a reduction, and no other body of workers in the transport industry have had their pay reduced.

Then describing the reactions of NSFU men on the *Orbita* and other ships, he continued:

As the days passed it became evident that the unrest was growing. Non–unionists and members of the NSFU, together with men attached to the AMWU, were insistent upon an opportunity being afforded them to discuss the matter. As a result of this the AMWU called a meeting of seamen.

The meeting, he said, was not confined to AMWU members and after the position was explained to the men they were left to decide policy. The resolution came from the body of the hall and since then no man at Southampton had accepted an engagement. Even the crew of the *Majestic*, signed last Friday, had given notice and left the ship. Scabs were brought in but some refused to sail when they heard the position. Although the *Majestic* had now sailed, he said, none of the original crew were on the vessel. In this he was correct: later reports indicated that the ship sailed with a depleted crew, although it was joined by men waiting on board a tug off the Isle of Wight.

As a counter move to the sailing of the *Majestic*, the AMWU called out their men on the cross-Channel ferries, and called for a restoration of the wage cut. Consequently, on the evening of 2 September Southern Railways warned the travelling public that 'owing to a general strike of our seamen, there is no possibility of any of our boats sailing from Southampton to-night'.[26] Ferries from Dover and Folkstone were not affected because, it was reported, seamen at those ports were not members of the AMWU.[27]

However, as with the larger ships, scabs were easily found and even on the evening of the 3rd some ferries sailed from Southampton to the Channel Islands and France. Without assistance for the seamen in France or on the islands, the strike across the Channel was soon over. But in the ports of Britain men were coming out, and this led to an acrimonious press attack on the seamen and on the AMWU. Shinwell was a particular target of vituperation with anti-semiticovertones, being variously described as 'the ex-tailor's presser', and 'Shinbad the Sailor'.

The press in Liverpool was particularly offensive. The article in the *Daily Courier*, of September 3rdwas typical of the daily outpouring. Under the heading 'Red Agents in the Ships', the article spoke of 'small but desperate bands of malcontents' trying to hold up the ships. Special watchmen and detectives on the staff of steamship companies were assigned to watch the berthed vessels. One company official referred to fire hoses in the docks as guns at the ready to stop pickets and was reported as saying: 'We have got to watch these pickets as we would watch rats ... We shall stop them at any price from getting into the engine–room, because some of them are very desperate'.[28]

The *Courier* also printed a long statement from Colonel H Concanon, joint chairman of the White Star Line, asking the press to inform all seamen that their actions abroad was mutiny and rebellion in the case of ships at home. Furthermore, if the strike were successful — 'an unthinkable possibility' — it 'would have a serious effect on industries throughout the country'. He concluded a long statement by reasserting that all boats would sail and that the strikers were being duped.

Dissension Over Tactics

When the leaders of the AMWU decided to back the seamen's strike it must have seemed to some that this was their one opportunity of winning the support of the majority of the men in the merchant marine. This was the event, announced by Shinwell at the July conference, for which they should be prepared to 'take advantage'. He had been loudly cheered then and here was the opportunity. The AMWU called for the restoration of the wage cut, for the removal of the PC5 and the reconstitution of the Maritime Board. These were obvious demands. The exclusive right of the NSFU to sit on the NMB and the operation of the PC5 card had to go if the union was to be reformed, or the officials replaced.

The AMWU, despite the legitimacy of its complaints against the NSFU, was by no means innocent of subterfuge. The most serious matter involved the tugboats. Without these craft the ships could not have got to sea and many scabs needed by the captains to make up their depleted crews could not have been moved onto the ships before they sailed. Yet, throughout the strike the AMWU refused to call out these men. The agreement with the tugboat owners was separate from that of other seamen, they argued. More to the point (although apparently unknown to the NMM) the AMWU would have come into conflict with the firms who had given them their little 'PC5' agreement. On 12 September the *Worker* criticized Shinwell for not pulling the tug-boat men out, and on the 14th the Central Strike Committee criticized the AMWU in a strike bulletin because it was organizing its own pickets. It also said of the tugs of one of the companies:

We further pointed out to the National Officials that if they are in this dispute to win, that the tug-boat men who are manning the *Sun* tugs should cease to tow the liners into the river, as elementary trade union principles demand that they should cease this work . . .[29]

Despite this the AMWU's complaints over NSFU policy needed an answer. Yet in line with Lazovsky's policy the NMM opposed the demand that the officials of the NSFU had to be replaced, and objected to the attacks on Wilson, on the grounds that the AMWU was only interested in 'poaching' members. In retrospect it is difficult to find excuses for any of the parties concerned. The NSFU's activities before and during the strike were reprehensible; the AMWU had undermined its claims to openness by boasting that they had their own PC5 arrangement with the tugboat companies and the NMM with its convoluted Profintern policy wanted no splits in the NSFU, irrespective of the rights or wrongs of the situation.

In a cat and mouse game inside the striker's camp the AMWU set up their own office in London, organized their own pickets and established a cafe to which striking seamen were invited. There they were offered free refreshments and their names and addresses were taken. The CSC advised the men to take the refreshments, but to proffer false names and addresses. Within a very short time the refreshment centre was closed![30]

The View From the 'Top'

On 3 September 1925 a special meeting of the Executive Council of the Shipping Federation was convened to discuss the strike. The Council members were well informed — their objective being to assess the strengths and weaknesses of the seamen's actions and to prepare for the coming period of confrontation.

Cuthbert Laws, the General Manager of the Federation, opened the session with a report saying that the strike had not started until the 12th of August. From the viewpoint of the 'agitators', he said, the strike was well conducted. 'Picketing was severe and intense' and this had intimidated a large part of the workforce in London, where two out of three were now afraid to sign on. Crews had to be taken to the ships at night and many men had to be brought in from other areas.

From London the action had moved to the Tyne, 'and for a time it was pretty fierce'. However, the Federation was active in the area and crews were recruited. Now the situation was quiet and men were being dispatched from this area to other ports 'at great expense to us'. The trouble had spread to Liverpool and then Southampton, and 'from their point of view they are attacking the right class of ship, but without any great success'. The Federation was 'trying to provide for an adequate supply of men by pooling the men throughout the country'. There were sufficient men and the only difficulty was to get them where they were needed — many being 'got at' and intimidated. However there had been no serious detention of any vessel.

Laws produced a list of every speaker engaged in the strike, 'and had his antecedents looked up'. In ninety per cent of cases, he said, they were 'pure communists' and the leaders of the trade unions were communist leaders. He singled out Hardy who he said was 'conducting the movement very ably'. Laws spoke of 'other forces' involved including the Clerks and the General Workers Union and of the opportunity being 'too good a one to be lost by Shinwell and people of that class . . . knowing very well that the communists will do the dirty work for them most efficiently'.[31] He described Shinwell as 'a man of pre-eminent ability', but said that the AMWU had probably less than 80 per cent of its claimed 8,000 membership.

Laws maintained that most ports were working normally (with ratings supplied by the Federation where required). One obstacle was the existence of the dole which made men 'very capricious'. However it was doubtful whether more than ten per cent of these were employable. He then turned to the situation abroad. In Australia the shipowners had been careful not to inflame a situation. Consequently 'after considering the matter very carefully', the Federation 'felt that the only thing to do was to remain quiet and not give any instruction to prosecute or anything of that sort'. They were still being cautious and, not wishing to cause friction, their agents had given the seamen 48 hours within which to return to work with a promise that, if they did return, there would be no victimization.

However in South Africa, where there was no local union, there had been an immediate decision to prosecute and it was only the government's request for a round-table conference that had delayed the issue. Now the time had come to do something in Australia, because the men had taken no heed of the employers' call for a return to work:

> We have been most patient over this. We have had a mutinous lot of men who simply declined to work and refused to move their ships. We having been as patient as we were it seemed to me the only thing to do was to endeavour to proceed to the utmost limit of the law with them.

Two further matters were raised at this meeting. Firstly, the chairman referred to the fact that the Australian seamen's leader might set up an opposition union in Britain and secure a large following. If he did so and succeeded, 'we might eventually have to pay Australian wages here on British steamers'. Sir Walter Runciman replied that the NSFU was working in harmony with the Federation and were fighting 'these other fellows in Southampton and we ought to stick by them and I think we will stand by them'.

The other matter referred to the wireless operators. They had not accepted the decrease of £1 in line with other seamen. The Board had temporized on this issue, and having originally said that the decrease would take effect from 1 September postponed it until 16 September. After discussion it was decided not to move until the present strike was over. With that the meeting closed.[32]

True to their decision, the Federation took no immediate steps against the wireless operators. But the agenda for the decrease across the board had been decided by the shipowners and, when the seamen were defeated, the operators would be dealt with. The offensive was total and nobody would withstand the employers for long.

4

RACISM AND THE SAILORS

White Sailor vs Black

Clause 3: Abolition of Chinese and Asiatic labour west of the Suez Canal.
Clause 7: British seamen to have the first right of employment on British ships, without interference to men who are already employed there.

> Programme and Prospectus: AMWU, June 1925. [1]

I was leading my storm troops (sic) to the back alleys which house the Chinese Laundries and Boarding Houses . . . A good many of the dives caught fire that day; quite a lot of Chinamen got hurt . . .

> 'Capt' E Tupper, on the 1911 Riots.

The man who talks of [racial] equality [among seamen] is not a Socialist; he is simply crazy and beyond hope.

> Forward, 11 April 1914

Race conflict is one of the less palatable aspects of working class history in Europe. It takes many forms, from prejudice through to race riots. Although not everybody was so tainted, the phenomenon is either overlooked or relegated to stories of the colonies. Yet the British labour press carried several items before the First World War that both reflected and fuelled the racism of the time. In 1914, one of the more radical socialist papers carried a full front page article by J O'Conner Kessack entitled 'The Case Against Lascar Sailors on British Ships':

> Economic facts alone, putting all ethnological questions aside, account for the prejudice against the black man . . .
>
> The Coloured man's life is low, his food simple and inexpensive and his clothing so scanty as to be financially negligible. He costs the Capitalist a mere fraction compared to the white man. He is squeezing the white man out. This is the real Yellow Peril. The standard of life is in danger, and the white man must either fight the evil influence or go under and carry white civilization with him.
>
> This explains much of the African row. Capitalism has a great unquenchable thirst for cheap labour power and much profit. White men instinctively realize it, and we have just seen the preliminary skirmishes of the great battle which will determine whether African and Asiatic shall displace Whites.
>
> *The man who talks of equality in this respect is not a Socialist; he is simply crazy and beyond hope.*[2]

The tirade continued (and there was a follow up in the next issue). Kessack had found statistics which he said showed the seriousness of the problem. There were 47,211 Lascars and Asiatics on British registered ships in 1912; compensation for injuries or death to these seamen, if paid at all, was negligible, meals provided were inferior and often made from discarded food and so on.[3]

Black sailors were caught in a Catch 22 situation. Those who signed on at a colonial port were accused by British seamen of depressing wages while those who sought a berth in Britain, where equal pay was available, were accused of depriving local men of jobs. This racism, which was ubiquitous, assumes importance in our essay, because seamen were confronted with the issue in Australia and South Africa in 1925 when they walked off their ships in protest against the wage cut. In Durban they were seemingly unperturbed by a virulent anti-Indian campaign that merged with support for their cause and in Australia their supporters would comment:

> Inchcape, Lord of the Lascars, has decided that in future all his coolies must wear spats as a mark of respect for [Prime Minister] Bruce![4]

This racism was neither new nor unexpected. It permeated the western world as it did the colonies. Seamen, squeezed by the shipowners and feeling insecure in the face of Asian and black competition, were as racist as their peers. This led to their participation in race riots in 1911 and 1919 in Britain. Furthermore, they expressed their protests against the employment of Chinese and Asiatic labour in the merchant marine in their union programmes.

The racism surfaced in several articles during the strike. In October a 'Ships Officer' wrote about 'Lascar Seamen in British Ships'. There he claimed that the many ships which sailed during the strike had crews invariably composed of Lascars or other Asiatics. This was only a half truth, as will be shown in chapter nine, but prejudice and 'truth' sit uneasily together. He thought that the publicity attending these sailings was good, because it exposed the 'disgraceful state of affairs in the British Mercantile Marine':

> The wholesale employment of Asiatics has two reasons — one being, that since they are in no way organized, they can be used with comparative ease as strike breakers. And the other that they are much cheaper than white men. British seamen, nowadays are intelligent men who have a pretty good idea of what constitutes habitable accommodation and proper food. Not so the wretched Lascars, who will live anywhere, and anyhow on the meanest fare imaginable — curry and rice, for instance, conveniently made from the saloon table scraps that would otherwise have to be thrown overboard.[5]

The statement this far is absurd and proof against rational argument or against fact.[6] But what followed was even worse. The employment of these Asiatics, said the 'Officer' was 'a grave menace to the safety of life and property'. In the event of a crisis at sea, he maintained, the Lascars were either unable to understand the officers' orders, or were too excited to do what was required, or would 'not greatly care whether the "white masters" sink or swim'. Nor would such men be concerned 'with the time honoured tradition of "women and children first"'. These factors, he warned, should be known by the Australian public, because they were 'being regularly carried to and from the Old Country in vessels that are largely manned in this way'.

A Background of Rioting

Racism and race riots are often manifestations of deeper social cleavages and most particularly of unresolved class conflicts. In times of severe economic deprivation, of widespread unemployment or of strike action, a section of the working class is easily diverted from its main objective and turns its anger against a minority group. This was certainly the case in the two race riots in which seamen were involved in 1911 and 1919.

In 1911 south Wales was racked with strikes: in the coalfields, on the waterfront and its support industries, in the ports and on the railways. Some of the anger that gripped the men was turned against shopkeepers, and Jewish shops became a particular target for attacks.[7]

The seamen's strike in Cardiff started peacefully and few scabs got past the pickets, in which blacks were prominent. The violence escalated as the days went by and, as more scabs were brought in, tempers rose. Yet, in the first stages, there were as many whites and blacks among the strike breakers, as there were Chinese. It is not our purpose to justify any scabbing, but it must be noted that Chinese seamen were not accepted into the union.[8]

The permanent Chinese population of Cardiff, of whom the majority were seamen, numbered less than two hundred. The other Chinese residents owned twenty–two laundries and a number of small eating houses. Nobody in this community played any part in the strike of 1911 yet, when the shipowners threatened to use Chinese scab labour to break the strike, they were attacked by the local population.

On 7 July the Cardiff Trades and Labour Council called for a boycott of Chinese laundries. Two weeks later (20 July) over a thousand whites swept through districts in which there was a Chinese presence and gutted Chinese laundries and other property. It was reported in the local press that well into the night gangs of men, boys and girls paraded through the streets, cheering and singing.

Like many such events, there were men available to egg the rioters on. Edward Tupper, friend and confidant of Havelock Wilson and leader of the strike in Cardiff, claimed in his memoir, that:

I arranged for a great demonstration to take place outside Roath Dock Yard ... All the available police mustered at what was to turn out to be a very orderly meeting. [Meanwhile] ... I was leading my storm troops to the back alleys which house the Chinese Laundries and Boarding Houses ... A good many of the dives caught fire that day; quite a lot of Chinamen got hurt ... But there were little white girls, some no more than thirteen years old, running out of the places.

We cleared the decks — and the Chinese laundries shut up shop. We let go over this job, and I confess my conscience never suffered ... England's conscience wasn't bothered anyway. I received thousands of letters — many from the Church — blessing us for this bit of riot.[9]

'England's conscience wasn't bothered . . .' wrote Tupper — and in this he was probably correct. But it is doubtful (as Evans argues, 1988b) that he led the rioters. Tupper was in court when the first riot took place, and the seamen were there to support him. He might have approved of the riot, but there is no evidence to link him or the strikers with the action that followed. However, what is significant in the light of his bully-boy tactics was his retrospective claim that he led 'his storm troops' in action. In 1938 he proudly linked his attitude with that of the nazis.

Racism and national bigotism were rampant during the war years.[10] The natural target for hatred was the 'enemy' and anti-German feeling led to assault of individuals and destruction of property — and even the disembowelling of Dachshunds! This xenophobia found new life after 1918, with stories that Germans were still plotting the downfall of Britain. The net of hatred spread to include Jews and then blacks, leading to the extension of the war-time Aliens Restriction Act in 1914 in 1919. During the parliamentary debates foreigners were accused of white slave trafficking, unnatural vice and pimping. [11] These attacks, false and provocative, resonated in the country, particularly in areas of high unemployment. Inevitably the seamen, and particularly black seamen, were drawn into the fray.

Eight thousand merchant seamen joined the armed forces, many of them black, recruited directly from the colonies. After the war they were left unemployed. This led to the setting up of repatriation committees, on which the NSFU was represented, in the seven main ports (Liverpool, Cardiff, South Shields, Hull, Salford, London and Glasgow). Their task was to persuade black seafarers to 'go back home' but they proved ineffective and were disbanded.[12]

In December 1918, a seaman from British Guiana, who had served Britain through the war, wrote to the Colonial Office from Cardiff:

We do not want any favour all we want is fair play. Every morning we go down to shipping offices to find ourselves work so as to make an honest bread and are bluntly refused on account of our colour. Whereas foreigners of all nationality get the preference. This is not only Cardiff but throughout the United Kingdom . . .[13]

In the months that followed thousands of Arab, African and Caribbean seamen sought work in vain, finding that officials of the NSFU or of the stewards' and cooks' union, were inciting crowds of white seamen against them. This led to the first Tyneside riot in February 1919 in which Arabs fought white seamen in South Shields.

From April to June there were race riots in Cardiff, Glasgow, Barry, Newport, London, Manchester and Liverpool. Seamen were not alone in these riots but they played a prominent part. In Liverpool events started with fighting between Scandinavian and black seamen followed by a police raid on boarding houses used by the latter. Then the mobs attacked. The men defended themselves with pokers, revolvers, knives and razors, but were usually routed. In one incident, a Bermudian, Charles Wooten, formerly a fireman in the Royal navy, was pursued and left to drown by a rampaging mob. There was also an attack on blacks in the boarding house maintained by the Elder Dempster Shipping Company.[14]

After 1921 came the depression. Trade declined, unemployment hit the coloured communities and seamen were badly affected. There were calls for restrictions on 'aliens' from the police, immigration officers, Poor Law Guardians and the NSFU. Each of these bodies wanted tighter control of men whom they described as law breakers, a burden on the community, a menace to the health of the community and an unfair competition to British seamen. NSFU officials demanded the repatriation of Arabs and tighter control over entry to Britain.[15]

The introduction of the PC5 card in 1922 affected the coloured seamen. They were not accepted by the NSFU as members and this prevented them getting a berth in many ports. There is some evidence of a trade in forged PC5 cards and of bribery for places on ships[16] — but the extent of this traffic remains unknown.

These pressures against coloured seamen in Britain increased and even long-time residents had to produce 'unimpeachable evidence' of being British subjects in order to stay. By 1925, with NSFU backing, 'aliens' were required to register through the Special Restrictions (Coloured Alien Seamen) Order. Men were also forced to register as aliens after police reportedly destroyed passports and other documents and then used the Order to deport them.[17]

Coloured Crews in the 1925 Strike

In their concluding passage of the *Analysis of the Shipping Industry*, the Labour Research Department addressed the issue of racism and said: :
... the attempt to exclude Asiatic labour has failed, and the campaign for 'equal rates' has only succeeded to the extent that the Maritime Board has granted equal rates on ships taking on Asiatic labour for the first time. The method that has not been tried is unionization of Asiatic labour. If this were done and a blackleg–proof organization achieved, the seamen's union would not merely be able to resume the struggle with the employers on far stronger ground; they would also be able to begin the creation of an International Seamen's Union, and so join all other workers in the struggle against international capital.

This comment, written about two years before the strike of August 1925, was a warning that was not heeded. The issue of racism in the ranks of the working class was important and its continued existence could only weaken the trade union. Given the strength of the shipping combine in 1925, only an international working class movement could have wrung concessions from the employers. But the call for an International Seamen's Union was not envisaged outside the ranks of the fading syndicalist movement and a few socialists. The NSFU under Wilson, Tupper, *et al* was incorrigible, and there was no move towards widening the seamen's union either through international links, or by organizing local coulered labour. Nor did the AMWU change its position on these issue. In February 1925, Cotter writing in the *Marine Worker*, launched an attack on the 40,000 Chinese, Lascars, Goans and Arabs who worked on British ships for 'dirt cheap' wages. This, he said, was unfair competition at a time when there were 30,000 British sailors out of work. To add to the problem, said Cotter, Clause 2 of the Anglo-German Commercial Treaty would give German seamen equal rights to be employed with British seamen on British ships.

Cotter had gone back to the NSFU by August 1925, but the AMWU did not alter course. It was therefore left to the unofficial strike committee in London, in August 1925, to invite Lascars and others to join them on platforms at meetings and, in Cardiff, centre of so much racial strife, the strike committee had no racial barriers. But that could only be a token gesture as long as the seamen's unions in Australasia maintained their own rigid colour bar. In Australia, in particular, several ships with all-coloured crews and even with mixed crews, defied the call to join the strike, and inevitably acted as strike-breakers.[18] However it is not clear whether race was the determining factor in their refusal to strike.

By one of those quirks of history, racism in South Africa assisted the seamen in the initial stages of the strike. There, the conservative whites of Durban opposed the recruitment of Lascars in India, because they would not tolerate their recruitment as scabs to replace white seamen. The government of the time (a coalition of Nationalists and Labour) with its rigid colour-bar philosophy also made it known that it would not allow lascars to enter South Africa. These pronouncements might indeed have bolstered the seamen in their strike action, but it did not lead to victory.

5

SOLIDARITY ABROAD

The Dispute Aboard the SS Inkum

On Monday 17 August 1925 a deputation from the crew of the British Steamer *SS Inkum* approached A C Woodfort, secretary of the South Australian branch of the Federated Seamen's Union (FSU) in Adelaide. They sought backing in their dispute with the captain of their ship and assistance if they took strike action. The *Inkum* had been chartered by the British Phosphate Commission as from 25 June 1925, the day it had left Newcastle for Nauru, and loaded for Wallaroo and Port Adelaide. The crew wanted Australian seamen's pay and conditions of work because, they said, they were engaged in coasting trade in Australian waters.

In 1923, Australian seamen won pay rises that set their monthly wage appreciably higher than that paid in Britain before the August cut. The disparity, said the *Australian Worker* of 26 August, was large, and even after adjustments for differing costs of living, the British seamen were grossly underpaid.[1] Not only were conditions for seamen on the British boats considerably worse, they were paid some 60 per cent of the Australian rate.

The crew of *SS Inkum* said they could not accept a lower rate, which would undercut their Australian fellow workers.[2] Assured of support should they decide 'to take drastic action' they pressed their demands and, failing to get satisfaction, resolved not to sail. The Master of the *Inkum* then offered payment at Australian rates from 25 June to date. He would not extend the higher rates until the end of the charter, nor accept the crew's new demand that the one pound deduction in their wages be restored. The waterside workers were asked for support but refused and would not assist the British crews.

The crew of the *Inkum* thanked the local FSU executive, saying:

> If [they] only had officials of their union as sympathetic to their wants as was now shown to them, there would be no fear of what would happen in regard to rates of pay and their working conditions.[3]

On 20 August the crew of *SS Woron*, sailing from Nauru to New Zealand also under charter to the Phosphates Commission, stopped at Fremantle and demanded Australian rates. Some men abandoned ship and got local backing. Unable to find replacements, the Master was forced to accede.[4] Five days later the British seamen in New Zealand joined the strike.

The *Balranald* was the next British ship to stop at Adelaide and, two days before a strike was called for all Australian ports, the crew asked for a hall in which to meet. There they decided, independently of events elsewhere in Australia, to strike and, with the backing of the Adelaide men, they demanded that the wage cut be restored.[5] At an enthusiastic meeting, H McKee (later elected chairman of the strike support committee) said:

> ... he must congratulate the overseas Seamen on their action, as it was clearly shown that they were waking up to their position as wage slaves. It was the grandest action taken by them ever since the inauguration of the National Sailors and Firemen's Union of Great Britain to overthrow the present bludging (*sic*) officials off their backs to obtain freedom. [Furthermore] it was their duty to not only reorganize the Union, but to organize for the One Big Union of Seamen of the World. When that day comes, we will see the dawn of a new era.

The audience, now including men of the *Zealandic*, responded to the warmth of these greetings and men of the *Inkum*, complaining that their union officials had always betrayed them, said 'they had been browbeaten and threatened by these sabotagers (*sic*) with unemployment if they mentioned any of their grievances'.

Woodfort was delegated by his branch to devote all his efforts to the striking crews and, sheltered and supported by the local union, they stayed ashore. Attempts by the Master of the *Inkum* to hire local tugs to move his ship were countermanded by the union. This was 'the first action implicating the Federated Australian Seamen in the British seamen's strike'.[6]

On 24 August, one week after the men of the *SS Inkum* sought help in Adelaide, the crew of the *Apolda* also demanded local rates. When this was rejected the men refused to sail. This ship was chartered by the South African government to carry timber railway sleepers in the west Australian trade. It had stopped at Bunbury, a major timber-exporting port and the crew, a mixture of Australians, South Africans and Britons — recruited under South African terms — were encouraged by the West Australian secretary of the Australian seamen's union to demand Australisn wages and work conditions. He interviewed both crew and captain and although none of the men belonged to the union they refused to sail. Shortly thereafter British seamen who reached Durban and Cape Town walked off their ships. The strike had reached South Africa and continued officially for one and a half months. The original crew of the *Apolda* were prosecuted in Australia and then black-listed by the South African government. The ship did not sail until 4 November when the strike in South Africa was finally over.[7]

The Threat of Deportation

Woodfort, addressing the crews of the *Inkum*, *Zealandic*, and *Baldranald*, spoke of a threat of 'deportations' said:

> He would remind the overseas seamen that never mind what the powers that be said, whether they deported Walsh, Johnson, Woodfort, or any, it must not shatter their solidarity to win. Whoever gets deported, it must not break the strike ... The deportees whoever they may be would desire to think, you were

[not] so weak to cave in, by the mere fact of some union official getting deported.[8]

The audience knew what this meant. Australian seamen, involved in a long quarrel with the shipping lines and the government, were smarting over recent legislation. Under the newly-amended Navigation Act, Australian conditions of employment were no longer mandatory in the coastal trade and the government was empowered to deport anyone who was not Australian born and tried to 'disrupt' the trading or industrial life of the community.

The FSU had been on the left of the trade union movement in Australia since 1919. It was then that the seamen, increasingly dissatisfied with the arbitration system (which was a barrier to their securing better working conditions) had come out on strike. They demanded higher wages, better sleeping accommodation on board ship and compensation when vessels were in quarantine. Tom Walsh led the strike which lasted for over three months. The seamen won a 35s increase in wages, a cargo working bonus, and increased pay for overtime work. Walsh was fined and imprisoned for three months for his part in the strike.[9]

Although victory was won by 'direct action', the FSU did not often employ the strike weapon, preferring to use the Arbitration Court to secure their demands. Walsh's reputation as a 'red' was also problematical. Born in Ireland in 1870, Walsh had been a member of the union since 1894 and its secretary since February 1918. He was a founding member of the Communist Party of Australia (CPA) in October 1920 and the seamen's union had been a mainstay of the CPA until 1923, when he fell out of favour with the party's leadership.[10] Nonetheless he offended the authorities by challenging the one shibboleth held by all Australian politicians — the belief in a White Australian policy and he roused many tempers during the British seamen's strike by saying that men who had fought in the World War had been fools for volunteering.

The FSU challenged the government's decision to sell its loss-making Commonwealth Shipping Line, acquired during the war, saying that the ships would fall to foreign flags: Australian conditions of work would no longer apply and local seamen would be replaced by foreigners. The conflict came to a head over 'job control', or who was responsible for the employment or dismissal of men and particularly, said the union, over the chartering of ships in Britain, under inferior conditions and lower wages than those operating through the Arbitration Court Award.

In 1925, before the British seamen's strike, the FSU came into conflict with the authorities. Walsh was fined £150 for incitement to strike when the union rejected a Court decision on where seamen should be 'picked up' for work. This was followed by wild-cat strikes. In early June the crew of a ship chartered by the Australian Shipping Board was gaoled for refusing to work after being denied Australian rates of pay and conditions of employment. Its cargo was transferred to two other ships and these were boycotted by the FSU. Although the Shipping Board went to the Arbitration Board the men refused to man the ships.[11]

On 5 June 1925 the Shipping Board and the Commonwealth Steamship Owners Association successfully applied for the de-registration of the FSU. The union, hampered by its lack of legal power to enforce its rules as a federal body or collect dues from its members, had to cut back on many of its activities. Defiantly, it claimed that it was strengthened by being freed from the fetters of the Arbitration Court and demanded that, in the absence of Court assistance, award conditions be incorporated in ships' articles — thus ensuring their protection under the Navigation Act. This was rejected by the shipowners and on 14 July Walsh ordered the men out.[12]

In response, the Nationalist-Country Party coalition government, led by S M Bruce, pushed the Bills (suspending provisions of the Navigation Act, and expediting deportations) through both houses in marathon sessions.[13] The Australian Labour Party (ALP), appealing for industrial harmony and consensus politics, fought the Bills at every stage. It opposed union bashing and criticized the ship owners and the combine which controlled the marine trade. The tenor of the ALP position is apparent in the minuted contribution of one of the ALP's more radical members, Frank Anstey, who said:

> [The bill's] purpose is to break those industrial organizations and destroy the conditions which have been won for our seamen, by permitting vessels manned by any class of labour to trade from port to port upon our coasts. I do not ask who are in the right or who are in the wrong, but if I held a position of responsibility I should endeavour to place myself in the position occupied by the seamen and find out what is the cause of the dispute. What has been said against the seamen may be quite true. A trouble like that which threatens can spread like a pestilence through the community and carry desolation to thousands of homes. It may wreck industry on farm and in factory in every state of the Commonwealth. What is the Government doing? ... Cannot the Government rise above the viewpoint of the seamen and of the shipowners and do something to bring about peace, unity and concord? I realize that for the proper observance of the laws there must be discipline among our workmen; but if the government seeks the public good, it will endeavour to remove the cause of this discord...[14]

Labour MPs and Senators turned on Walsh and the leaders of the union. One ex–miner, Senator J E Ogden (who voted with the government on this issue), attacked Walsh for advocating revolutionary politics, for his policy on strike action and for denying that working class interests could be secured through the Arbitration Court.[15] Others were both xenophobic and racist.[16] The Navigation Act, said Senator E Findley was 'passed to protect the seamen of Australia against underpaid and overworked seamen of other countries' and the government was sacrificing the White Australia policy.[17] In the debate this view was expanded:

Senator Pearce: The first trade unionist in Australia to repudiate the White Australia doctrine was the secretary of the Seamen's Union.

Senator Findley: The employers of Australia were the first to declare against a White Australia. At an inter-state conference of employers a few years ago, the president said in effect, 'We want immigration. As we import commodities we should import labour, be it black or white'. We do not object to any one because of his colour, but we do object to a man of alien race, unaccustomed to our habits and our civilization, coming here unless he complies with the conditions that apply in Australia. So far as coloured seamen are concerned, we know they get the wage the white man gets, so long as they belong to the union. We also know that the objective of those that believe in having any sort of Australia, black or white, is cheap coloured labour, imported under conditions which are a disgrace to any civilized community.

Behind this argument — that it was the wage level and not the colour issue — the defence of the White Australia policy was obvious. Coloureds (Chinese, Japanese, Javanese and blacks) were not wanted in the country. Senator A A Hoare, also of the ALP, argued that the legislation would 'allow coloured crews to compete on the Australian coast with Australian seamen'. These, he said, would be confronted by waterside workers who would refuse to handle their craft. He saw the legislation as 'a danger to the White Australian policy' and added: 'We shall not allow boats that are manned by coloured crews to engage in the inter–state trade of Australia'. Then, switching to Labour's other voice on this policy, he added: 'Those crews receive the "magnificent" wage of 10d per day'.[18]

The ALP position was summed up by E Riley at the end of the debate in Parliament. He moved that the Bill be 'properly described by its title . . . "for the encouragement of the employment of black labour in the shipping industry"'.[19]

The passing of the Navigation Act Bills opened the way to the deportation of the seamen's leaders, but the shipping trade was brisk, and shipowners accepted a compromise, negotiated by the Melbourne Trades Hall Council. The Union surrendered its claim to job control and accepted penalties for crews who delayed the sailing of vessels; the employers agreed to incorporate the former pay award terms of employment and pay wages fortnightly.[20] There were no deportations, but the threat remained. When British seamen came out in August a Deportation Board was appointed to report on Walsh and Jacob Johnson (or Johannsen as he was called by the press to stress his foreign origin).

The Strike in Durban

Men walked off three ships in Durban two days after the start of the *Apolda* dispute. They said they would work in port but would not sail unless their grievances were attended to. Further reports indicated that other crews might join them.

There were no South African shipowners and shipping lines had not established local branches there. Mailboats, passenger and cargo ships all had their headquarters in Europe. Consequently, there was no sizable corps of seamen in South Africa and the small Sailors and Firemen's Union, based only in Cape Town, played little or no part in the strike. With no seamen's organization to offer assistance to the strikers, the shipping companies and their agents felt no constraint in issuing summonses for mutinous behaviour.[21] Two men were arrested by the Commanders of the *Sandgate Castle* and *Balmoral Castle* in Durban for refusing to obey the lawful commands of the Master. They appeared in court on 28 August and were sentenced to fourteen days imprisonment with hard labour, suspended for two weeks subject to their immediate return to duties.[22]

This precipitated the strike in Durban.

Further court proceedings were halted when the South African government, a coalition of the National Party and South African Labour Party (SALP) decided to arbitrate in the dispute.[23] This did not stop further crews walking out and Durban was soon clogged by ships that could not be moved. The strike spread to Cape Town and, with stoppages in East London and in Lourenco Marques, there was only restricted sea traffic between the South African ports or between the country and the outside world for forty seven days.[24]

There was unrest in Durban when the news agency Reuters reported on 1 September that the Union Castle Line was recruiting 700 Lascars in Bombay to replace existing crews. It was not unusual for shipping companies operating South African lines to use Lascars and they had already manned one of the chartered ships in Australian waters with a crew that was 75 per cent coloured.[25] But there was fury in some sections of Natal, where anti-Indian feeling was rampant, when it was disclosed that Lascars would be used as scabs against white crews. It was claimed that the shipping companies lost the public support they had previously enjoyed. One observer was reported as saying that Lascar crews would eventually take over all cargo vessels, 'but to introduce strike breaking crews at this present time is a different matter'.[26]

At this juncture H H Kemp and Dan Simons, both with a history of involvement in earlier South African labour struggles, intervened. Kemp, one-time assistant town clerk in Durban, and member of the municipal union, had been victimized in January 1920. The municipal workers walked out for three days and all civic services came to a standstill. The (all-white) municipal workers set up a board of control ('Soviet' it was called) which was installed in the town hall. Within the day Kemp was reinstated and a permanent conciliation board of councillors and employee s established.[27] Kemp was a member of the Labour Party until May 1924 but was expelled when he stood against and lost to the party's nominee in the general election. After his defeat he called for the formation of a new party that would exclude all Asiatics from South Africa.[28] During the seamen's strike, in September 1925, he sent a cable to the Prime Minister on the recruitment of Lascars, saying:

> Durban feels virtually as one man on this subject. Ugly situation will arise. Would recall to your memory events of 1897 at the Point. Remember on this occasion there will be no Harry Escombe to thwart public will ...[29]

Simons had been a Labour Party town councillor in Benoni in 1911. He was employed at the New Kleinfontein mine and was on the miners' strike committee in July 1913. When the mine management refused to make any concessions a general strike was called. General Smuts summoned the (British) Dragoons which shot at random into the assembled crowd, killing 30, and wounding over 200.

Nonetheless the government was forced to retreat and the miners were victorious. Simons was heard of again when he supported the railwaymen's strike in January 1914 and was detained for a short period under martial law.[30] He is known to have sided with the pro-war majority of the SALP in 1914–18 but there were no further reports of his activities until he reappeared in Durban as a supporter of the seamen. By then he was crippled and sold tobacco and cigarettes from his wheel chair near the Gardens.[31]

Daily meetings were called at the Durban Town Gardens to put the sailor's case to the public and this forum was dominated by Kemp and by Dan Simons. There was a large crowd at the first meeting and, according to press reports, Simons 'neglected his business' and organized a collection for the six men due to appear in court the next day. Thereafter he was appointed President of the Durban strike committee and presided at all meetings in the Gardens. At the second meeting the audience was reported as 15,000. Kemp, who was the main speaker, reminded his audience that he stood for the expulsion of all Asiatics from South Africa. If Lascars came, he said, he would lead the citizens of Durban in throwing them into the Indian Ocean.

Other members of the SALP and the white trade unions brought messages of solidarity but Kemp dominated the gathering and rallied the widest support, always stressing his racist line. When he spoke to (white) railwaymen and mentioned the Lascars and his previous anti-Asiatic campaigns, he was greeted by cries of 'Bravo Kemp' and 'Up Boys and at 'em'.

Kemp's call for Indian repatriation was neither unique nor original: it was the policy of all white parties in South Africa including the SALP. Measures to force repatriation were placed before the Natal Provincial Council and South African Parliament in 1923–5. In 1924 Indians in Natal towns lost the municipal franchise and their right to buy or lease land. Then compulsory trading and residential segregation were proposed by Patrick Duncan in his Class Areas Bill. With the defeat of the government at the general election in June the measure fell away.

Dr D F Malan, the new Minister of the Interior, reintroduced the measure as the Areas Reservation Bill in mid-1925 with even more stringent clauses to restrict Indian rights. After the Indians of Durban held mass meetings against the Bill and called for a Round Table Conference to discuss their position in the country it was shelved, but it remained a permanent threat to Indian rights and the community remained insecure.[32]

During the strike the South African Indian Congress (SAIC) expressed 'deep regret' over the planned use of Lascars as scabs. They likened this move to the original importation of indentured labour in the sugar estates of Natal, leading to anti-Indian campaigns: and they urged 'responsible leaders of India' to denounce the shipping companies.[33] At a Cape Indian Defence Committee meeting speakers were more damning. They warned Lascars to stay away as this 'was purely a white man's dispute, [because] ... both sides, in their capacities as voters when on shore, were parties to the repressive legislation passed under the British Crown against their Indian fellow-citizens'.[34]

With reports of Lascars being recruited and on their way Indian organizations grew ever more apprehensive. Amod Bhayat, President of the Natal Indian Congress, cabled 'prominent persons' in India:

Community here disapproves such action as unfair to strikers, and further
complicates present Indian problem. We implore you keep Indians out of
this strike so preserve Indian honour. Suggest recall any Lascars already
left.[35]

Abdul Karim of the Natal Indian Association cabled the Viceroy of India and
Pandit Motilal Nehru on similar lines, saying:

Arrival Lascars South Africa this juncture when all minds agitated new
Asiatic Bill disastrous Indian interests. Local Indians strongly resent Indian
seamen exploited as strike breakers totally condemn action shipowners rush-
ing to India unmindful serious issues involved. Pray recall Lascars.[36]

There was concern in India. An editorial in the *Times of India* of 3 September
condemned the recruitment of scabs, stating that they could be hurt and warned of
unpleasant consequences for the whole Indian community in South Africa. The
General Secretary of the Indian Seamen's Union referring to the rejection of Lascar scabs during the shipping strike in China, asked officials of the All India TUC
to stop any recruiting for South Africa.[37]

Whether Lascars were ever recruited is uncertain. The *Times of India* carried
conflicting reports: that inquiries had been made about the availability of Indian
crews from local agents of shipping companies; that such crews could be supplied;
and then silence.[38] If attempts were made to raise the 640 scabs the Union Castle
line was said to have requested, they were never sent. The South African press carried copious reports and rumours on the matter. The Nationalist paper *Die Burger*
was quoted as saying that 'Public opinion will not permit it, and we fear it will
merely give rise to undesirable emotional excitement and even to worse things'.[39]
Prime Minister Hertzog received hundreds of telegrams from across the country
protesting against the use of Lascars as scabs, and the Cabinet response was that:

Under the law, Lscars, being Asiatics, are prohibited immigrants, and the
Master of the ship bringing such persons to a port of the Union is ordered to
retain such persons on his ship and to remove them from the Union, failing
which he is subject to heavy penalties. Landing for temporary purposes or
trans-shipment is not permitted without the consent of the Immigration
authorities. The Government has received no information from the
shipowners, who are well aware of the law if any such step is taken as that indicated by Reuter's telegram.[40]

The issue was dead. When it was reported, on 17 September, that Lascars on
ships involved in the strike in Durban were fraternizing with their white colleagues there was no noticeable reaction.

6

ALL OUT IN AUSTRALIA

The One Hundred and Two Days

The strike of the British seamen in Australia extended from Wednesday 19 August through Saturday 28 November: a total of 102 days. On 20 August, over 1,000 British seafarers attended a mass meeting at the Communist Hall in Sydney and voted unanimously to strike in all Australian ports until the one pound cut was restored. Walsh presided and was reported as saying:

> If you are prepared to let the owners take the vessels to sea when they like, you are a lot of 'hot-air merchants'. If you are determined to obtain what you are justly entitled to, refuse to leave the ships. Even if you are sent to gaol there is no need to worry. You will receive no wages, but you will get food and shelter.[1]

The following morning a larger meeting affirmed the decision to strike and repudiated Wilson and the officers of the NSFU. They resolved 'to elect representatives and re-establish the Union on a firm basis when we reach England again'.[2] Men spoke bitterly about conditions at sea and said they could see no reasons for working longer hours at sea and in port and receiving less pay then Australian seamen.

There was an estimated fleet of fifty British ships in Australian ports and with one exception (the *SS Chitral*) all those in Sydney and the three ships in Brisbane remained strike bound. Walsh encouraged the men in their action. He promised them the support of the FSU and this was seized upon by the British union and the shipowners. Havelock Wilson and the NSFU attacked Walsh both before and during the strike. On 8 May 1925 *The Seaman* accused Walsh and his colleagues of being Communists who had hounded out the previous officials of the union because 'they were not Bolshies', and of subsequently leading the seamen astray by their provocative tactics.[3] After the strike spread to Australia, Wilson was vitriolic in his attack: the stoppage was a 'red plot', he thundered, the seamen 'were not union men' and Walsh was blamed for all that happened. On 24 August the *New Zealand Times* printed the text of a cable Wilson sent to Walsh:

> Your conduct in interfering with the men on British-owned ships is treacherous and dirty, in view of the fact that you sent me a telegram asking whether I would recognize the transfer of any members of the Australian union to the British union on this side. By your unreasonable conduct you have destroyed the prestige of the Australian Seamen's Union which was

built up by able men. You have betrayed your trust, and I suppose you hope to destroy the British Seamen's Union.

Wilson also called on Prime Minister Bruce to prevent Australians illegally intimidating British seamen or persuading them to repudiate the wage agreement.[4]

On Saturday 22 August, over a hundred men from three British vessels in Melbourne (the *Portfield, Cornwall,* and *Port Kembla*) joined the strike. They stayed on their vessels to avoid charges of desertion and to supply steam for the working of the winches. Crews at Brisbane and Newcastle also stopped work, lending support to the men already out, but widening a rift inside the seamen's ranks. At least six ships in port with coloured crews (although some had a large complement of whites) refused to strike.[5] On Monday the Marine Transport Group gave its full support to the British seamen's action — but because the strike was unofficial, representatives of the Transport Unions called for more information from Melbourne and Britain. A strike fund was started with a contribution of £150 from the FSU, and a weekly levy of 5s imposed on all members until the strike ended.[6]

The strikers, lacking a centralizing strike committee, faced new problems in some ports. Three hundred men of the *Themistocles* were locked out and had to find places to sleep and in other ships food was not available because the cooks were themselves on strike, or because there were no rations on board.[7] Arrangements were made by the FSU for feeding the men in Sydney at the railway refreshment rooms; shelter was found in union halls, at the Communist Hall and in the homes of trade unionists. Further funds were donated by the Labour Council of New South Wales.[8]

However, there were new moves against the strikers from the shipowners, the government and the press. On Monday some British shipping companies received the names of those who had ceased work from their Australian representatives and stopped the men's families drawing any allotments. At the same time British mail was directed to Australia via America in an US steamer.

The Australian cabinet met and commissioned three of the ships of the Commonwealth Line to carry wool abroad and, on 24 August, the Governor–General Lord Forster proclaimed 'a serious industrial disturbance prejudicing or threatening the peace, order, or good government of the Commonwealth'.[9]

The press followed suit. An *Argus* editorial on 25 August, aimed at Walsh and Johnson, said:

A few evilly disposed persons, resident in Australia, but not born here, are endeavouring to paralyse overseas shipping. Should they succeed, the injury to Australia will be incalculable. Indeed if an enemy in war sought to employ the means most injurious to Australia he could not have found anything better for his wicked purpose than those destructive measures which are being attempted. If such an enemy won command of the seas he could not have cut away our means of living more effectively. The enemy within the gates can succeed only if Government fails. One or other force must prevail. Victory would go to the revolutionaries if it could be conceived that the Government was not able to govern . . .

The leader writer called for the deportation of these 'evilly disposed persons', condemned the strikers for attacking the trade union leaders of Great Britain and called for the recruitment of scabs to get the ships sailing again. Such 'volunteers' would be the true proponents of 'personal liberty' [no less], and 'really upholders of the British unionism which the misguided men now on strike have repudiated'.

On 28 August the government moved to apprehend Walsh and Johnson but were blocked by J T Lang, the Premier of New South Wales, who would not allow state police to serve the Commonwealth summonses. A Special Strike Police Bill was rushed through both Federal houses establishing a special corps of federal officers.[10] The *Westralian Worker* of 4 September, in caustic comment, denounced the government:

> Down to the seventies there came from the old world to this country men who had learned in suffering the bitter lessons of the shackles which privilege had imposed on liberty. Crofters from Scotland, Fenians from Ireland, and Chartists from England, hopeless of reform in the land of their nativity, came to the Southern Cross in thousands. Many came because there was no alternative . . . Here they vowed to make things new . . .
>
> Now the great tradition is in a process of reversal. Association with an industrial combination to prevent a wage reduction is declared a crime . . . To be an Englishman is to be a potential deportee . . . And to what avail? All the transportations ordered by Peel and Lord Melbourne did not arrest the growth of trade unionism in Great Britain; whatever deportations Bruce and Page effect from Australia will not paralyse the functioning of the workers' organizations in respect to the fight for social betterment.

Walsh and Johnson were arrested and brought before the Board to show cause why they should not be deported.[11] On 21 October their deportation was ordered but, on appeal, the High Court declared (on 11 December) that Walsh had no charge to answer, because he was in Australia before federation and Johnson had been in the country long enough to place him beyond the reach of the immigration laws.[12]

The First Negotiations

One week after the strike began in Australia both sides had assessed their position. There were some 2,500 seamen on strike and it was their action — not that of Walsh or Johnson — that determined the position. The forces opposed to the strike included the shipping agents, the Bruce government, the conservative press and sections of the working class like the stevedores (who would not support an unofficial strike). Coloured crews on many ships in port stood aloof and were prepared to sail if they could get the cargoes and the help of tugboat men. The press was still down-beat its leader writers spoke about the problems that dairy farmers would face with the butter export season about to begin. If the existing favourable conditions continued, the weekly surplus available for dispatch would be 100 tons. This would grow rapidly until the end of September, when the surplus would be 550 tons per week. Other farmers were not yet threatened. Wool and wheat were coming onto the market and supplies would continue to grow. However, to date, non–British ships had no difficulty in taking the cargoes aboard and unless the strike continued for a lengthy period there did not seem (at the time) to be much concern about future shipments.[13] On the other side stood the Australian seamen and many dockers, the local trade unions, the Communist Party of Australia (CPA), the small socialist groups and (with some reluctance) the ALP leadership.

Then came reports that State Ministers had arranged for a deputation from the strikers to meet agents of the British firms on Thursday 27 August. The men, who had no authority to represent the strikers, demanded the restoration of the one pound cut no victimization and the settlement of the dispute through the offices of the FSU. However, the British shipowners cabled their representatives to say there would be no departure from the rates of wages and conditions decided by the National Maritime Board and rejected any settlement through the Australian Union. The talks were over.

As the strike took effect new difficulties were reported. On 29 August the mail was declared 'black' in Queensland and bundles of letters lay in the railway stations. The sugar industry was said to be paralysed and in some districts cane cutting was suspended. Commodities were said to be nearing exhaustion. In towns near Brisbane, for example, flour, sugar and butter were unavailable.[14]

Meanwhile there were difficulties with which the strikers had to contend. There were defections in the ranks: some men did not believe in striking, others responded to distress signals from their wives and families and they signed on for a passage home. Those that stayed faced hardships as the strike lengthened. On Wednesday, 2 September, the agents demanded that all men on strike report for duty within 48 hours. The shipowners promised to waive their legal rights against the strikers and, because the men had been misled there would be no victimization. However, if there was no return within the specified time, these conditions would be withdrawn.[15]

The ultimatum was ignored but on 12 September the *SS Surrey*, the first ship to raise anchor after striking, sailed from Melbourne with a full complement of men. All accepted the reduced rate of pay. Before it sailed the Master, H G B Fields, addressed the Deportation Board, providing the 'evidence' of a conspiracy in Australia to bring about a stoppage on British ships.[16] He said that those members of his crew who joined the strike on 19 and 22 August, did so under instruction from the FSU.

Such tactics (connived at by government and press) were a cause of concern in radical circles. The *Westralian Worker* on 25 September said:

> ... the papers have concentrated their attacks on various Union leaders, and by constantly stressing their short-comings have tried to impregnate the public with the idea that the whole trouble is caused by the unreasonable demands of these individuals ... many people are judging the merits of the dispute according to their personal opinion of the seamen's leaders. And thus does the paid press fulfil its allotted function.

Sometime in September the Masters of vessels began charging the men with 'having refused to obey lawful commands'. On the 9th, 329 warrants were signed in Melbourne. There were few difficulties. The seamen generally co-operated with the police, saying that this would relieve the strike fund the need to pay for their upkeep and that conditions in gaol were better than those aboard ship. When the men appeared in court four days later a large contingent of supporters participated in a sympathy march, including railway refreshment waitresses, who were themselves on strike.[17] The strikers marched behind banners that proclaimed PRISON BEFORE SLAVERY. — HEROES IN 1914, SLAVES IN 1925.

The seamen pleaded not guilty. When the magistrate asked whether they would return to their ships and take them back to Britain, they answered in chorus, *NO!* They were sentenced to three weeks imprisonment and fined two days' pay. But not all suffered arrest calmly. One seaman, confronted by two detectives at the Central Railway Station, escaped. He was pursued, but other seamen followed and there was a punch-up in the street before a third policeman appeared brandishing a service revolver. The man was arrested and charged.[18] On the 12th the *Leader* also reported that the shipowners would issue summonses to the 500 men on strike in Melbourne, that a large number had been issued in Adelaide to be followed by another 300 in the coming week.[19] Two men from the *Port Kembla* were arrested in Melbourne and would be charged with disobedience. Thereafter, arrests, charges and prison sentences proceeded continuously. On 19 September the *Leader* said that 946 warrants had been issued in Sydney and many seamen had been arrested without resistance. In Adelaide over 200 men had been charged and more summonses had been issued.

The strike also revealed strains on the waterfront. Walsh urged the Waterside Workers Federation to support the strike, but could not win them over. Furthermore, Walsh's differences with Johnson[20] widened during their joint trial. At a meeting of the FSU, Johnson, supported by much of the leadership, accused Walsh of going against FSU policy by advising the British seamen to use the Arbitration Court to present their complaints. Walsh, in a spirited reply, said that he had only advised the men to exhaust every avenue of securing their demand. Most of the leaders claimed that Walsh had acted unwisely, but a vote of no confidence was lost by a large majority.[21] A second issue, appearing in many newspapers, was not confined to a single meeting. It was reportsed that a section of the strikers wanted to launch a new union in Britain with Walsh as president. Walsh was ambivalent declaring that, if the union were formed, he would be prepared to consider the proposition. Johnson opposed the move, claiminf that a new union would be isolated. He urged strongly that the project be dropped and that the seamen work from within the NSFU to change the leadership.

Stalemate on the Waterfront

Through September and October the press bemoaned the transfer of cargo from British to foreign vessels, 'buried' the strike or wrote about a communist conspiracy. None were real issues. Speaking about the 'loss of freight' to

British shipowners, J H Scullin, an ALP member of the Federal Parliament, condemned the 'hum-bug' spoken about British ships competing with foreign ships of it being well known that they worked in unison. When the wage reduction was agreed, he said, British and foreign shipping companies all increased freight charges by 10 per cent. He claimed 'that the freight on wheat from Australia shipped during the coming season has been increased by 4s per ton. This increase would pay the seamen's wages three times over'.[22]

Of the second point, the *New Zealand Worker* (9 September), said that the strike had died so often that it was not certain which action was being talked about in the press. How far these reports emanated from deliberate mis-information put out by the shipowners is not clear, but (as the paper commented) any intelligent editor should have noted that there was a remarkable repetition of the same falsehoods. The *Westralian Worker* on 4 September also commented on the conspiracy theory, so widespread at the time, in a satirical piece:

> *Who held up the British ships in Brisbane?*
>   *Tom Walsh!*
> *Who held up the British ships in Port Adelaide?*
>   *Tom Walsh!*
> *Who held up the British ships in Melbourne?*
>   *Tom Walsh!*
> *Who held up the British ships in Fremantle?*
>   *Tom Walsh!*
> *Who held up the British ships in London?*
>   *Tom Walsh!*
> *Who —! —! ?? ***?*
> *Who —!!! —??? —ssz —ssz ****
> *—!!!! —?*
>   *TOM WALSH!*
> *Gug–gug–gug–gug–sputter, fizz–z– +*
> *thud!*

> *I'll 'old 'is 'ead. Ring up the ambulance, somebody.*

Caring for the Strikers

The men on strike were thousand of miles from home, separated from their wives or families, without money, housing, food, tobacco and drink. Furthermore, after the initial excitement of taking industrial action, there was little to fill the long hours. This was a potential hot-house for radical ideas and for hatching plots. Both their supporters and their opponents knew what this involved and, in tandem with shipowners in Britain, some ships' captains took steps to insulate their crews from the men ashore. In October, when *SS Orvieto* arrived in Sydney, it was reported that she was anchored in the harbour instead of the wharf and all shore leave was stopped. Only persons with the agent's or the captain's permission were allowed aboard. Also, when it was thought that the men might join the strike, an amusements committee was appointed, a canteen installed (undoubtedly with plenty of beer) and concert parties, dances and cinema shows arranged.[23]

For the men ashore, food and entertainment were arranged by local strike committees, comprising socialists or communists, members of the FSU, and representatives from each ship. They raised money, arranged billeting, paid for meals, and provided pocket money. The striking seamen learnt how to speak at street meetings, or at workshop and factory gates and at weekends there were dances — with music provided by crew members.[24]

The situation seemed ripe for communist intervention and yet, despite accusations of communist conspiracies from government and the press, the CPA played no significant role in the strike. Not one official of the Australian Seamen's Union was in the CPA,[25] and their marginal position on the seafront was underlined when they called, quite unrealistically, for a general strike as the only means to prevent the deportations. An editorial in the *Workers Weekly* of 28 August declared under the heading 'To Arms Workers!' that the only answer to deportation was to:

... stop every wheel, every tram, every train, every ship. Paralyse the commercial system of Capitalist Australia. Answer their violence upon the Labour Movement of this country, by a similar attack upon the flow of profits.

The CPA, at loggerheads with Walsh, lambasted him in a *Worker's Weekly* editorial on 11 September. Maintaining that the government had deliberately transferred the struggle 'from the industrial field into the filthy channels of "Legalism"', it commended Johnson for declaring that: 'the fight was not one of deportation generally, but a section of the working class — the British seamen — in deadly grips with their oppressors'. The CPA claimed that capitalist courts could be used by workers in the class struggle, 'not by prolonging the proceedings in the time of crisis by long, wearisome and useless argument on legal technicalities, but by stating a fearless class position ...' The deportation case, it said, was overshadowing the seamen's strike and was sidetracking the class struggle. Walsh was not mentioned, but the implication was clear: he was *persona non grata*.

Yet Walsh, writing to the Waterside Worker's Federation, asking them not to handle blacked ships, made the same point as Johnson. 'Deportation', he said, was 'a very secondary consideration':

The Bruce government is ... determined to carry out its deportation policy, but as this matter arises out of the British seamen's strike you will see the importance of winning the strike ... if deportation is to be eventually defeated, it is essential to win the strike first. The removal of one or two men is a very small matter when compared with the importance of strike [action] to the working class. This is the first time in the history of affairs that the British seamen have attempted to make themselves really articulate. They have at last revolted against a corrupt oligarchy composed of their union officials and the British shipowners.[26]

Yet there was no obvious reason for favouring Johnson. On 26 September the *Leader* reported that speaking on a CPA platform, he had criticized his hosts because they were not revolutionary. He also attacked the ALP because it was prepared to act as the administrative body for the capitalist class and condemned the 'busy-bodies' who could only assist Bruce in winning the election by trying to organize a general strike.

Johnson's criticisms were, perhaps, of little consequence. The overwhelming problem was the fate of the striking seamen, isolated and in a 'no win' position. The shipowners were prepared to wait and time was on their side. Writing in the *Australian Worker* on 23 September the columnist H E B[27] said

So wealthy is the Shipping Combine that it doesn't care how much the breaking of the strike costs. Whatever the expenditure involved, the men must be ground under the iron heel of mastership.

Towards the end of September the level of frustration rose and the seamen grew restless at the lack of progress in their cause. The problem lay not only in Australia, but also in the changed momentum in South Africa and the ineffectiveness of the strike in Britain. On 23 September the *Australian Worker* reported that 41 British vessels were held up in Australian and 13 in New Zealand ports. There were 13 ships at Sydney, 11 in Queensland ports, 10 at Melbourne, five in South Australian ports, four at Fremantle. At this stage Matthew Charlton, leader of the ALP in the Federal Parliament, persuaded overseas shipping representatives to meet the strikers in conference, together with members of the Trades and Labour Councils and waterside workers. But the strikers would not meet the employers until all imprisoned men were released and the one pound was restored. They also called for the blacking of the *Snevic* and the *Orvieto* which had left England after the commencement of the strike.[28]

Responding to an electoral challenge from Charlton, Bruce dissolved parliament at the end of September, and called an election for November. This was condemned by the *Westralian Worker* (25 September) firstly as an attempt by the government to turn the strike to its advantage, and secondly as a means of denying men who were appearing before the Deportation Board, or (in the case of British seamen) appearing before the Bench, a fair hearing, despite the fact that the cases were *sub judice*.

On 26 September the *Leader* stated the government case:

... constitutional authority against communism, the most important question of the moment ... brought to a climax by the present shipping troubles and the threat of further industrial disruption followed by a hold up of the export trade ...

The government feels convinced that 'foreign communists' and 'disruptive elements' are defying the law with impunity, and that they are becoming daily more dangerous.

It was these circumstances, and not the deportations that were at issue. The real question before the tribunal had been smothered in legal arguments and technicalities.

Nonetheless, one further attempt was made to bring the parties together. On 13 October, Mr Justice Powers, President of the Federal Arbitration Court, called for a conference to end the strike. This was rejected by the conservative press, which maintained that Australia had no official standing in a British strike.[29] The shipowner's stated their position in *Fairplay* on 15 October. If the seamen had any justifiable grievance, they wrote, the place to complain was in Britain, where there was 'ample machinery for their protection'.

Under no circumstances, however, will they allow themselves to be forced by men who have been either misled or coerced by local extremists into making any settlement in the Commonwealth at variance with the agreements signed individually for the voyage ... A settlement on any other basis would be subversive of law and order, and entirely opposed to the accepted methods ... by which wages are regulated.

Nor are the shipowners unmindful of the serious effect upon the convenience and facilities of the Australian public, and especially upon their export trade, of a state of affairs which is not the shipowner's creation, but has been brought about by a small and irresponsible group of the Australian community ...

Being upright people, they claimed, they had tried conciliation. They had even offered to waive their legal rights and could do no more because that 'would place a premium on bad faith'. Even though they were suffering great losses there were principles at stake:

If the shipowners should acquiesce in their violation, the result would only be to buy not peace, but constantly recurrent turmoil and uncertainty. Should extremists in Australia be allowed to hold up vessels, or seduce their crews, in defiance of their agreements and their own union into holding them up, it will manifestly become impossible to carry on maritime communications ...

Violence in the Closing Stages

For refusing to carry out duties assigned to them, the strikers faced fines, arrest and imprisonment and, as the strike dragged on, seamen attacked scabs brought in to get the ships moving. However, the violence came mainly from those who opposed the strike, and those who were most hit by the absence of transport. They counted their losses and bemoaned the shortages and the farmers were furious at the failure to move their produce.

The biggest onslaught on the seamen and their local supporters was reported along the coast of Queensland, from Brisbane to Cairns, a distance of over 900 miles. In late October strikers from the *Mahia* in Gladstone (some 300 miles north of Brisbane) ejected six graziers from a steamer and the jetty, fearing they were scabs being smuggled aboard their ship. They rejected the captain's story that the graziers were attending a 'social evening'. The crew picketed the gangway and also moved and scattered the contents of eleven trucks of coal which the captain said were 'to enable the refrigerating machinery to be kept going'. The next day some

150 farmers gathered — and threatened to increase their numbers to 500 — but were persuaded by a local politician that the captain would get the coal aboard.[30]

The same issue of the newspaper reported that the position in Cairns was desperate. The *SS Hopewell* had left the port without loading logs, 24 trucks of sugar and trucks of produce. Business in the city and the district was almost at a standstill and the position was worsening. It is felt, said the report, 'that some sort of action is imperative'. This was already being organized, although the parties behind the 'imperative' action seem to have maintained a discreet silence. Farmers from the coastal towns were being mobilized to converge on the town and take the law into their own hands.[31] They had the obvious support of the right-wing press. The Herald's comment was, 'extreme elements [were] expected to oppose the farmers'! Finally, it was reported, some 600 farmers picketed the wharf, and routed strikers who tried to prevent eighty waterside workers loading the vessels under protection.[32]

There were parallel events at Bowen where 250 farmers collected to load coal and sugar on the ships. Their first attempts failed because railway drivers refused to allow the transport of coal.[33] Attempts by farmers to manhandle the trucks were prevented by the police because they were the property of the Commissioner of Railways. But then there was a policy reversal: one driver was suspended for refusing to transport coal from the railway yards to the jetty and eleven additional drivers were drafted in. On 4 November farmers began loading sugar on the *Port Hardy*. As a consequence, the Bowen railway line was declared "black" and for several days it seemed as if the railway men would walk out. The millworkers at Proserpine also reacted to the farmers' action by calling for strike action. However both railwaymen and millworkers had recently concluded strikes and the workers were in no position to resume their actions.

The matter did not end with the loading of the ship. To press acclaim, the farmers swept through Bowen on 6 November, 'cleaning up communists and extremists'. The report said that thirty-five 'extremists' were dealt with, half applying to police stations for protection: 'the more dangerous remained in custody on charges of creating disturbances'.[34] Farmers warned that they would take drastic action if trouble was revived by 'extremists and obstructionists' and they also took action to protect those waterside workers involved in loading the ship. They had, in fact, gone too far. The workers were incensed and the trouble only subsided when it was reported on 14 November that the farmers had agreed not to bring a blacked ship into port and would not work such a ship if it entered the port.

In the final stages of the strike there are several reports of incidents in Fremantle giving a picture of turmoil in the docks. The first event involved the captain of the *Demodocus* who tried to move his ship with the aid of his officers. When the striking seamen learnt of the move they stormed the ship, drew the fires and placed a guard in the engine room.[35] Other reports that day stated that the captain and officers were threatened with violence if they resisted.[36]

A more serious clash is described in a retrospective account by Leslie Rees, critic, broadcaster and author, at that time a trainee reporter at the Fremantle branch office of the *West Australian*. Reporters met the boats, he said, looking for copy for the eastern State papers. They found considerable tension in the harbour because ships officers tried to get ships away by removing hawsers from the bollards. On one such attempt, a ship with a depleted crew did manage to sail and this led to a storm of protest.[37]

It was dangerous to walk down the quay because strikers gathered to show their resentment against the officers by hurling metal bolts, stones and coal at the decks and portholes. Passers-by, said Rees, found themselves hustled, threatened, or showered by missiles and when a police officer tried to board the *Borda* he was assaulted. At 8.30 in the morning of 2 November, 103 policemen and mounted constables were mustered to assist the master to raise steam and move the ship. Seamen on board and police on the wharf confronted each other — until the mariners decided to disembark and charge. The policeman in charge described the situation as follows:

> As long as I live I shall never forget the firm confident and resolute faces of the NCOs and Constables when I told them to draw their batons and await the charge. It was a thrilling moment as it filled me with pride and confidence in the little band. A man amongst the strikers called for the bugler. After a couple of blasts intended for the advance the strikers roared charge. I waited until they got within a few yards and I gave the order to charge and words fail me to express how bravely the men responded to the call.
>
> It was a hand to hand conflict. Police and strikers falling in all directions. As fast as one of the force fell his place was filled with another, keeping the rank unbroken ... The field of action resembled a miniture (*sic*) battlefield several Police being stretched out with bleeding wounds while here and there were wounded strikers some lying on the wharf others staggering from wounds.[38]

After a brief truce to remove the wounded the battle continued. Reinforcements arrived for the police and after another charge the strikers were defeated. The Police Inspector described the event as 'one of the most serious affrays that ever took place in Australia'.

About a hundred strikers were arrested, brought before a magistrate, and each fined £2 for resisting arrest. Having no money they were taken to the cells but were brought back and released because, fortuitously, the strike had ended. A few hours later they were on their ships, preparing to sail.

The attitude of the Labour Party to the event, based undoubtedly on their dislike of Walsh, was to describe the strike as being supinely conducted.[39] The previous week there had been a fuller comment, and this too sums up the ALP approach:

> If Monday's disturbance was meant as an effective demonstration against the British shipowners, it turned out to be a ludicrous failure. Working class history of all countries is replete with examples of mass action against constituted authority. In all such instances there is abundant proof that governments have placed at the disposal of the employer the powerful resources of the state to smash organized labour. Wherever such demonstrations have taken place in Australia, the workers have been united, and have been represented by a strong representative executive committee of all trades and workers affected. The personnel of Labour in industrial disputes

of magnitude in the past have very often successfully resisted the encroach-
ments of the employer. The British seamen have been unfortunate, inasmuch
as they did not think it advisable to confer with the representatives of organized labour in this state with regard to tactics or the general conduct of
their campaign . . . Had they done this the Darktown disturbances on Monday would not have eventuated. Labour organizations in Australia have left
behind the ineffective protests of brickbats, stones and bludgeons. Such
methods are a reflection on the intelligence and humanitarian instincts of our
people.

The paper then contrasted the 'crude effort' on Monday with the previous good
behaviour of the seamen. Admitting the irritation at police patrolling the wharf,
the paper then stated:

Is it not far more desirable to have local police under Inspector Sellinger,
who has acquired a very high reputation locally for absolute fairness, and a
high conception of his responsible duties to Fremantle citizens . . . rather than
see the Bruce Commonwealth soldiery installed . . .

What the seamen answered is not known but in the aftermath of the events of
the night it would not have been very complimentary. On 13 November the
Westralian Worker accused the seamen of being 'indecisive, blind and
disheartened' and their leaders 'incapable of initiative'. But, said the paper, there
was still some backbone and some 200 men refused to join their ships 'until an effort was made to liberate their comrades'. It was the Trades Hall officials and not
the strike leaders who got busy expedited the slow processes of the law and got the
prisoners out of gaol.

The strike in Australia was officially called off on 26 November 1925, when the
seamen's representatives met the shipowner's agents, and accepted the terms
agreed to in Britain. But the dispute was partly renewed when the wireless
operators came out on 28 November and many ships stayed in port. This is discussed in chapter nine.

The Cost of the Strike

There was no final account of the losses due to the strike in Australian ports. In
his article in the *Australian Worker* on 23 September H E B had said:

Already, in Australia, the laying up of the ships, in harbour charges alone, has
cost the owners as much as would have paid the men the disputed pound a
month for ten years. And when to this amount is added the loss in freight and
fares . . . what the Combine has lost in this country alone exceeds what it
would gain in many years from the whole British service by the enforcement
of the proposed reduction in wages.

Yet it is prepared to go even further than that. Cabled advice states that the
shipowners contemplate stopping all sailings until the men are starved into
surrender.

On 2 and 9 December, the same paper gave the estimated loss of wages to the strikers as £80,000 and the cost of the strike to the shipping companies as two million pounds. Enough to pay 5,000 men the extra pound for 400 months, or a little more than 33 years. However, no comprehensive statement was ever presented on those costs or indeed on those incurred by Australian farmers, merchants, and businessmen. Even after the strike was over it was claimed that the losses continued to mount. The truth of this always remained obscure. The *Times*, 1 December 1925, explained that it was not practicable to bring all the ships home at once and that there was also a shortage of refrigerated tonnage for the transport of produce to Britain. Consequently ships would still remain idle in Australian ports for some considerable time. Round trips that should have taken four months had been extended to nine months — while overheads and losses in passage and freight earnings mounted. Furthermore, it was claimed that during the long strike many of the European lines had strengthened their position at the expense of their British rivals. Whether this was a real loss or a transfer inside the combine to shipping lines which paid even lower wages to the seamen, remains a moot point, but one thing was clear: there were even fewer berths for British seamen and many were forced to seek other occupations.

7

THE STRIKE IN SOUTH AFRICA

The Pact Government and the Strike

Economically, South Africa was badly affected by the seamen's strike. To maintain a favourable balance of trade it was estimated that the country needed an annual surplus of visible exports over visible imports of £15,000,000. The only substantial exports, besides gold and diamonds, were food and wool, and the optimum months for the export of the latter were from August to October. In 1925 plentiful rain and the control of pests and blight led to bumper crops after years of depression. Shipping delays were bound to have severe effects on local farming communities.[1] Maize and oranges due for export were stored in the ports or the countryside: the oranges in danger of rotting and the maize attracting rats with the added danger of plague.[2] Imported food, including flour, was in short supply, and more general imports — some ordered for the Christmas season — were threatened.[3]

Besides consumer goods, the mail to Britain was badly affected and business communications with the country's main trading partner slowed down. The cable, as was pointed out early in the strike, could not replace the postal service and was heavily overloaded.[4] Machinery needed by the mines was either held up in Europe or lay in the ships' holds in danger of rusting.[5] Gold was not exported; bunker coal for the ships was unsold; and ostrich feathers lay neglected in storage while the European market for this foppery collapsed.

In the first days of the strike business interests sought a means to man the ships and the *Eastern Province Herald* suggested that:

We must protect ourselves if wc can. We must span in the natives [who] ... would be glad of the work. They would do it quite efficiently at reasonable rates ... The stoking and stewarding of the steamers is a simple task and the natives could easily be trained to do it.[6]

The newspaper claimed it 'should be sorry to carry out such a change' but it would be necessary to stop the country's trade being brought to a standstill. It also said that General Hertzog might have trouble with his labour colleagues in the pact government but faced the alternatives of losing the season's citrus crop or offending the socialists. Initially the National Party opposed the strike and joined the NSFU in calling on the seamen to return to work. However, as republicans, they would not have responded to Havelock Wilson's claim that the strike was a plot by men who wished to break up the British Empire.

All negotiating was left to Colonel Creswell, leader of the SALP and Minister of Labour. Yet the dispute threatened to tear the party apart: Creswell wanted to end the strike and offered to mediate between shipowners and seamen while Walter Madeley and Morris Kentridge, leading members of the SALP, supported the seamen.

The Communist Party of South Africa (CPSA) and white trade unionists were also drawn into the conflict. CPSA involvement, like so many events of the strike, seems to have been accidental. Soloman Biurski, a member of the CPSA in the Cape states, in his unpublished memoir that having read of the strike in the local press he hurried to the docks with offers of financial assistance and a campaign to back the striker's demands.[7]

The Strike Spreads to Cape Town

During the first week only the white unions and the SALP supported the seamen. In Durban they provided money and comforts for the crews and, on 30 August, the Transvaal Labour Party Conference backed the strike, rejecting the government's support for the shipping companies. Creswell opposed the resolution saying that the seamen were duty bound to honour the agreement negotiated by their union.[8] There was another, unspoken, reason: the 'Pact' government represented both farmers and white workers and Labour ministers seemed more concerned with placating farmers than advancing the cause of labour.

Initially the Cape Federation of Trades, to which most (white) trade unions in the Cape Province were affiliated, spoke for the seamen. This ceased after A Z Berman, the acting secretary, announced that the Federation was approaching the Fruit Exchange (the government's co-operative marketing board) to arrange for the sailing of the *Roman Star* with a cargo of oranges.[9] He also said that the men were prepared to accept the restoration of the *status quo* pending the reopening of the whole question through conciliation or arbitration in Britain, and the postponement of the new rates pending such negotiations.[10]

The seamen, who had not been consulted, repudiated Berman and the Federation.[11] It was at this stage that Biurski of the CPSA met the men, suggested that they elect a strike committee and was appointed secretary.[12] Joe Pick and S A Rochlin, also members of the CPSA, joined the strike committee and strike headquarters were set up at the CPSA offices in Long Street. The party called daily street meetings to put the seamen's case to the public, collect money, arrange billeting and so on.[13]

On 22 September S P Bunting declared that at the Cape the strike

was being very largely and materially assisted, if not actually conducted, by the Communists, who were always associated with any trouble in which the workers' interests were at stake. The Communists took credit for that, and their object was to secure the unconditional surrender of the shipowners, which was the only possible condition of settlement ... The men were fighting for 8d per day, but as Communists we are supporting them for something more.[14]

The strike committee's first concern was the fifteen million oranges loaded in the specially refrigerated hold of the *Roman Star*. Berman and leaders of the Cape Labour Party appealed to the crew not to strike because the ship had been chartered by the Fruit Exchange and many fruit farmers would be ruined if the boat did not sail.[15] Other leaders of the SALP hastened to intervene. Creswell decided to mediate between shippers and seamen, while Madeley and Kentridge said they would go to Cape Town because of their concern about agricultural cargoes, if the seamen felt that as supporters of the strike their presence would help.[16]

On 4 September, Biurski announced that the seamen did not wish to be discourteous to the government and would therefore meet Creswell but that the dispute could only be settled in London.[17] In private discussions Creswell appealed to the strike committee to let the ship sail 'as a gesture to the first labour government (*sic*) in South Africa'. The men agreed, provided it was announced in every port that the committee had given its permission and that the ship returned to Cape Town with the same crew if the strike was still on. Creswell had no power to agree to the terms and, when a ballot showed that the men opposed the sailing, this agreement fell through.[18]

The *Roman Star* did sail but only after the crew, many of them strikers, were offered an extra £6 for the next year, much to the annoyance of the Shipping Federation.[19] During the voyage there was an explosion in the engine room when a detonator was shovelled into the ship's furnace and three crew members were injured.[20] The oranges were never delivered and sabotage was suspected. Biurski believed that it might have been the work of a fireman who burst into a strike committee meeting and said he was volunteering for the crew but they were not to think badly of him. However, despite police investigations, nothing was discovered.

Other consignments of oranges did not sail. There were reports that oranges worth £35,000 would have to be dumped in Table Bay and in Marico alone citrus growers and packers lost over £30,000.[21] Other produce was also held up: dairy farmers, forced to keep back butter and eggs, incurred considerable losses. Maize got away mainly on foreign ships.[22]

Creswell's attempts to mediate failed. He could have met some of the seamen's demands such as the release of strikers from gaol and a government guarantee not to tow ships to the outer anchorage, but other demands were not within his powers. The seamen wanted the one pound restored, the Maritime Board abolished and the exclusion of Havelock Wilson from the affairs of the British mercantile marine.[23]

The seamen could not have sustained their action if it had not been for the support they received while in port. One unexpected prop came from passengers on the *Ballarat*. This consisted mainly of migrants to Australia, many of them women, under a joint Commonwealth-State scheme and some Australian seamen travelling home. There were 'warm' relations between passengers and crew in the three weeks journey to Cape Town and the Australian seamen were probably 'crucial in steeling both militancy among the crew and sympathy among the passengers' The men of the *Ballarat* came out and the ship was in port for forty three days, being there from the start and remaining until the end. They also persuaded the crew of the *Arundel Castle* to join with them against the cut in wages and together they constituted the 'local fortress of dissent'.[24]

With no sign of an end to the strike the captains tried to get their ships out to sea. In one incident, which was to steel the resolve of all strikers, the master of the *Sophocles* locked his crew in the messroom and with the assistance of the officers got the ship beyond the three mile limit. The seamen were then ordered down to the boiler room and warned that non-compliance would lead to charges of mutiny. They refused saying that when at anchor they had declared they would not sail. Three hours later the *Sophocles* was back in port[25] and the crew called on everyone to stand firm.[26]

The End of the Road

There seems to have been little or no contact between the seamen in Cape Town and Durban. They had seperate strike committees but events in one port, as reported in the press, presumably informed the other.Nor was there a national union (as in Australia) to help co-ordinate the strike.

Seventeen British vessels were in Durban harbour in early September and 1,235 men were ashore (including 200 engineers, officers and others who were not involved in the dispute). After attempts to take the *Port Curnow* three miles out to sea where men were ordered to work or face mutiny charges, the men left the ships.[27] On 18 September, Creswell visited Durban to meet shipowners and men. He wired Hertzog that the men would not stay on the ships even though they said:

> We know that we are liable as prohibited immigrants ashore to be run in. We are quite prepared for you [to] put us in gaol or in detention camp under strict guard but we will not return [to] ship with risk be[ing] taken [to] sea as *Port Curnow* was. If owners will guarantee us against this we will return at once.[28]

The guarantees could not be given and further discussions proved futile. In the same telegram Creswell urged the government to remain neutral in the dispute, particularly as 'unanimous denunciation that [of?] Union by seamen as not efficient agent and uncontrolled by them'. He thought the government should charter ships to relieve the situation.

The shipowners and their agents were exasperated. Their standpoint, stated by the editor of *Fairplay* on 1 October:

> The position of the South African (*sic*) shipowners ... has been gravely aggravated by the action of the Government authorities, who, apparently, without inquiry into the merits of the dispute, sided with the strikers. If they had taken the slightest trouble to look into the case they would have found that under the agreements the men were bound to continue at work, and that, as a matter of fact, reductions and one advance had been made under them in the past and accepted without demur. Instead, however, of doing so, when

the strike occurred, members of the Government announced that, under the
Immigration Restriction Act . . . the strikers were 'proscribed immigrants',
thus rendering the owners liable to a fine of £100 if the men remained on
shore for more than six months, and to a further fine of £100 for allowing
them to land, and at the same time making them responsible for their keep.
They have thus directly contributed towards forcing owners into a loss which
at the best it will take years of trading to make good.

The editorial added that the Union Castle line would soon have to stop the sailing of mail boats 'from home'. Two weeks later a letter from a South African ship
broker was printed in *Fairplay* which showed that conditions on the ships were
appalling:

> . . . there is some appearance of an ugly spirit amongst the men, whose leaders
> have been wiring the Government saying if certain things are done they fear
> violence will result . . . the inner anchorage at Durban is . . . crowded, and all
> the seamen have to stay on board the ships, [leading] . . . to pollution of the
> bay, with all the sewage from such a number of ships.

This it was said had led to some ships being moved to the harbour entrance, but
the men 'had rushed to the engine rooms and drew the fires'. The ship broker
ascribed this to the fears of lying outside at sea with 'no chance to run ashore' but
he knew, as did the public at large, that the men were afraid of suddenly finding
themselves on the high seas compelled to work or face charges of mutiny.

The men who came ashore in Durban were billeted in the houses of sympathizers, occupied corners in work sheds or camped in open spaces. They purchased
food with funds collected by trade unions (including the black trade union movement, the Industrial and Commercial Workers Union of Africa, or ICU), and
Labour or Communist groups throughout South Africa.[29] But as the weeks went
by the situation in Durban worsened. Ships sailed with skeleton crews, or with locally recruited scabs and some British vessels manned by Lascars, or non-British
ships, loaded produce and sailed for Europe.[30] Still the men remained firm and on
24 September the Durban Strike Committee issued its ninth strike bulletin, rebut-
ting reports in the *Natal Mercury* that the committee had 'modified its demands'. It
claimed:

> These statements are deliberate lies. No reductions have been accepted and
> the strike committee has not, and does not intend to put these so-called
> proposals in front of the men. The whole thing is a dirty attempt to sow the
> seeds of panic in the ranks of the strikers . . . Immediate steps have now been
> taken to prevent any trickery of this sort being flung against us in the future
> . . . Ship committees have been set up on . . . vessels composed of delegates of
> the seamen and firemen in order to keep contact between the men on board
> the ships in harbour and the strike committee ashore. Henceforth every
> striker will know in detail how things stand . . . Meanwhile . . . every man-jack
> [is] standing fast . . .[31]

An increasing number of unemployed tried to board the ships. Pickets were
deployed near companies recruiting crews and were posted at railway stations as
far inland as Pietermaritzburg to intercept men being brought down by the ship-

pers. The press (and strike bulletins) reported increasing violence as men were prevented from reaching the ships. Meanwhile some captains were approached by men with intimations that they would welcome talks to end the deadlock.[32]

In Cape Town, where the strike was also nearing an end, there were insufficient billets although many families helped with accommodation. Assistance was sought from the authorities and the men were taken to the Wynberg military camp where, bound by minor restrictions, they became charges of the government. Ultimately some 600 men were in the camp under canvas, supplied with blankets, rations and cooking utensils.[33]

However ships got away from Cape Town in increasing numbers as men drifted back to the ships or as unemployed whites volunteered (at £9.10s per month) for service. The scabs faced a barrage of abuse, but they were defiant and generally impervious to the pleas of the men on strike.[34] At the end of September, the Cape Town correspondent of the *Times* reported that:

> The strike has now taken the form of a war of attrition in which, on the whole, the strikers are losing ground . . . Shipowners are getting ships away, and among scratch crews there is always a sprinkling of former strikers.[35]

A Labour 'Coup' and the End of the Strike

Except for the agitation over the Lascars, the strike was supported mainly by sympathetic whites in South Africa. White workers who rallied behind the seamen did not contemplate industrial action and at most the unions passed the hat around. The rumours at the end of August that African stevedores in Durban were discussing a strike were not heard again.[36]

A week later, James LaGuma, General Secretary of the ICU informed Clemens Kadalie, the President, that dockers were discussing strike action if their demands for better wages and conditions were not met. He also said the strike committee in London had sent a cable to the crew of the *Arundel Castle*, via the ICU office in Cape Town, stating that the strike was 'solid' in London and calling on the strikers to stay firm.[37] LaGuma continued:

> I have also been approached by several representatives of the seamen, or at least it has been suggested that we, the ICU should take up the negotiations on behalf of the seamen; but I pointed out the regrettable colour prejudice in this country and the fear that it would be detrimental to them by alienating the sympathy of the European public which they have strongly at present . . .[38]

Kadalie, however, offered to negotiate on behalf of the seamen, but agreed with LaGuma that after the strike there would be a large demand for dock labour to load the ships. He urged the implementation of the ICU demand of 1925: that all dockers be paid the same rate as then prevailed in Cape Town. No more was heard of the negotiations, although members of the ICU attended rallies in support of the seamen in Cape Town. There was no further talk of strikes in the docks.

The position of the strikers worsened. Large numbers of seamen were charged for disobeying orders and only stayed out of gaol pending appeals. For this, bail was needed and funds were not easily available. The trade unions provided considerable sums[39] and in late September, R (Bob) Stuart, Secretary of the Federation of Trades used this to 'invite' the strikers to switch their headquarters from the CPSA to his offices, and when it was rejected, threatened that financial support would be withdrawn.[40] The committee had no option but to move to the Federation offices.[41] Nonetheless when the Federation was criticized by seamen in a strike bulletin the strike money was immediately suspended. The committee thought of breaking with the Federation but then sought a compromise.[42]

The strike seemed dead-locked − but the shipowners and the NSFU would make no concessions.[43] There was a ballot in Durban at the end of September but only thirty voted to return to work.[44] However, the strike could not be sustained and on 10 October men in Durban agreed under protest to end the strike by 311 votes to 230, with the promise of no victimizations, no prosecutions, clean discharges and the customary opportunity of selecting the next voyage. Men whose ships had departed would be repatriated and would also get clean discharges.[45] The AMWU was consulted and recommended acceptance. On the 12th they called off the strike in Britain.

The London strike committee conceded defeat a week later but, with the men still out in Australia, the strike was only declared over in South Africa on 24 October. In November many seamen were still out in Durban,[46] but ships sailed regularly, stranded passengers had gone, produce and other goods were moved. Inevitably men were left behind, and in December some 500 to 600 destitute seamen were shipped home by the South African government.[47]

The Impact on South Africa

The strike was not of South African origin but for two months there had been strikers in the main ports and thousands of local citizens were involved. The South African economy was in difficulties: many farmers, including wool producers, faced disaster; the bank exchange rate moved against the local currency and gold awaited export. Yet few have left accounts of their reactions during or after the event.

There is almost no mention of the strike in the records of the Labour Party or of the Communist Party and filling the blank pages will not be easy. In Johannesburg a Seamen's Strike Relief Committee was set up, with Fanny Klenerman as secretary, W H Andrews as treasurer, Frank Glass and others who were in the SALP as members. They condemned the arrest and prosecution of strikers and tried to persuade tugmen not to tow 'scab ships' out of South African ports.[48] This brief news item conceals a story that needs unravelling.[49] Andrews and Glass, who were close friends, had been founder members of the CPSA and, with Klenerman, were active trade unionists. In May 1925, Glass had resigned from the CPSA and joined the Labour Party. Andrews allowed his membership of the party to lapse and Klenerman (soon to become Mrs Glass) was in the SALP. Working together with Madeley and Kentridge, the support committee was firmly in the hands of Labour, and the communists outside Cape Town were isolated.

Ultimately the strike failed, and failures lead to a loss of morale. Biurski, who had invested so much energy in the strike, was destitute and unemployed. The CPSA was a small sect and, unable to win the white workers, turned their attention increasingly towards the black labourers. The white unions gained little (if anything) despite their support for the seamen — and even this was blemished by the threat of fund withdrawal in Cape Town. The SALP showed from the beginning of the strike that it was split and this nullified some of the credit it gained for its part in the strike. It had been in the government for barely a year when confronted by the seamen's action and the division in their ranks was a warning of events to come. Among the Labour Party stalwarts who played a part in the events in Natal was Dr Minnie Alper who conveyed messages of solidarity, and provided money and provisions.[50] Kemp and Simons did not make the headlines again and their further activities are not known. In 1928 the SALP was torn apart: Creswell remained a supporter of the Pact government and Madeley led a minority who broke ranks.[51]

The Indian community was relieved of the fear that Lascars might arrive and make their position more uncomfortable. They continued their agitation for a Round Table conference and it was convened in 1927. Its outcome was not affected by the strike. What might have become obvious to more radical elements in the community was the timorousness of the leadership if indeed they needed further evidence.

The greatest impact of the strike was on the country's economy and whatever the tendencies in economic planning at the time, the event must have helped concentrate minds sharply on the physical isolation of the country. This had been obvious during the First World War, and was now brought home again. In the absence of a local fleet, the need to develop manufacture must have been obvious. We can only guess at the impetus this lent to plans to build up the steel and other industries. It is not necessary to propose that the strike was the over-riding factor, to see that it must have played some part in speeding government intervention in the development of local industry but it must remain a surmise until more is known of the impact of the strike on local thinking.

The group that had most to lose from a seamen's strike were the farmers who were dependent on British ships for the export of their produce. Despite calls from sections of this community for an end to imperial ties, the farmers would remain dependent on Britain — until alternative markets were discovered, or new methods of transport became available. Yet, above all else, the strike had demonstrated the tenuousness of the ties of Empire: it was control of the seas that tied the Dominions to Britain and the strike showed that this could no longer be taken for granted.

8

THE 'HOMEBOAT' STRIKE

The Strike in New Zealand

There was little or no contact between the seamen's unions of Australia and New Zealand but the strike that affected the Australian ports soon encompassed New Zealand. Ships bound to or from New Zealand joined the strike in Australia and men everywhere spontaneously walked off the ships. The strike began in Wellington on Monday 24 August and within a few days had spread to every port. Known popularly in New Zealand as the Homeboat Strike, it got considerable support from trade unions and socialist groups and was sustained for over two months.[1]

The division between conservative press and labour press, so pronounced in Australia, was replicated in New Zealand, with the right-wing newspapers vociferous in their red-baiting and denigration of the strikers. Items from the British press that claimed the strike was caused by 'communists' or, alternatively, that the strike had failed were repeated without question. On 24 August, the *New Zealand Times*[2] printed the cable sent by Havelock Wilson to Prime Minister Bruce in Australia repudiating Tom Walsh and condemning the 'Reds and with them the miserable number of non-unionists who are anxious to make the unionists berthless in order to supplant them'. In the same issue of the paper there were complaints that British lines were being supplanted by foreign ships. The reports were either uninformed, half-true, or just malicious. Other items claimed that in Britain 'men were signing up for all berths', ships were sailing or that 'in London pickets were molesting men returning to their ships'. The case of the *Orvieto* received much attention. This ship, it was reported, was delayed in London because the crew was on strike but men were being brought to London to replace them and the strike was 'not expected to last many [more] hours'. However it then transpired that many men brought in to scab on the *Orvieto* had refused to sail.

The Australian FSU was also lambasted. On 24 August, the day on which the strike spread to New Zealand, the *Evening Post* condemned 'Tom Walsh and his fellow-dictators in Australia ... [who] if they have not incited the trouble ... have certainly done their best to foment it'. It praised Havelock Wilson as 'an honest and steadfast worker for the seamen ... [who had] wrought a wonderful improvement in seafaring conditions'. Now he was being maligned by the local seamen because ... 'he believes in honouring agreements and is sensible enough to recognize that good union conditions must have a basis in the prosperity of the industry'. 'In any circumstances', said the paper magisterially, 'the agreement is made, and if there is to be any firm basis for collective bargaining it must be honoured'.

On 25 August the *NZ Times*, reporting the decision to strike in New Zealand claimed again that the strike was 'fizzling out' in Britain. Alongside this, the paper also carried an editorial that reflected the tensions building up in the Pacific region over events in China. Under the heading 'Directed from Moscow?' the editor wrote:

The *Daily Mail*, in a leading article, says that various ports of the Empire are at present being exposed to a formidable and concerted Communist onslaught, financed and directed from Moscow.

The Bolsheviks are using every kind of poisoned weapon. They concentrated the vague Nationalist upheaval in China into a furious anti-British boycott. They also aim at producing disaffection among the sailors and dock workers in Australia, Canada and Britain, in pursuance of a plan of specifically attacking ocean transport, from which Britain draws her lifeblood.

The plot to undermine naval discipline includes the sending of bogus bluejackets to harangue Hyde Park audiences on the alleged wrongs of the lower deck.

'The revolutionary hornets will not bleed the Empire to death', the paper says, 'but we must recognize the existence of a malignant conspiracy, backed by plenty of money and fertile brains, and take the requisite measures to crush it'.

Quoting further from the *Daily Mail* it said that the strike was a plot against the British Empire 'engineered by Communist groups, linked up with the Russian Soviet. In Australia British crews are being incited and terrorized by local Communists'. The *NZ Times* said of the strikers in Australia that they were in 'a parlous condition, foodless and shelterless, except for such assistance as is afforded them by the seamen's organization'.

The strike commenced in Wellington when the crew of the *Arawa* decided not to sail until the one pound cut had been restored.[3] The ship, already delayed by the crew, had been due to sail for Southampton the previous Wednesday with cargo that included fresh produce and a considerable number of passengers. A hundred British seamen and firemen also met in Auckland and, resolving to strike from the 25th, said:

That this meeting of members of the [National] Seamens and Fireman's Union of Great Britain and Ireland resents the treacherous action of the President, Havelock Wilson and other members of the executive for agreeing to a reduction of £1 a month in our already starvation wages. Further we insist that the rates of pay current in July last be paid to seamen in all orders, and that there be no resumption of work until these conditions are accepted.[4]

The *NZ Times* continued its offensive against the strike and painted a Manichaean picture of trade union practice. On the one side stood Wilson who could do no ill and opposing him was Tom Walsh, the devil incarnate:

Mr Havelock Wilson, moving on a different angle, reaches the heart of the Walsh position. He treats Mr Walsh as the tool of the extremists who respect no law and act always for Red revolution. For them any stick will do to beat the capitalist dog, even if the blows of the stick crumple up the cause of unionism. Mr Havelock Wilson convicts these interfering unionists — who are working without either right or knowledge — of treason to unionism. He proves that their pretence of loyalty to unionism masks their attack on unionism itself. Their loyalty stands convicted of devotion to another very bad cause.

Mark, in addition, the ingratitude of this most sinister proceeding. No man living has done so much for the British seamen of Britain directly and for the seamen of the whole world indirectly and consequently, as Mr Havelock Wilson. He has achieved a great success through all opposing influences, of bad report and malicious invention. Yet the moment he recognizes the inevitability of circumstances he is abused in the foulest manner.

Walsh and Co. profess to regard him as a criminal. Now his crime is the sane understanding of the situation, his adhesion to common sense, his determination to do the right thing as he, in his matchless knowledge sees it . . .

The seamen were defended by the *NZ Worker*[5] in an editorial that looked at the larger problem facing the workers in Britain. Unlike the British labour press the editor of this paper saw quite clearly the connection between the seamen's strike and the attempt by the employers to lower all wages.

At the moment when the British TUC supporting the Miner's federation was able to ward off cruel reductions in wages, and when it is clear that only by energy and solidarity can the British workers safeguard themselves against deeper impoverishment, Mr H Wilson . . . wins the plaudits of the profiteers press by accepting a wage cut of £1 a month on the semi-starvation wages of seamen on British ships . . . The wages he agreed to, namely, 45s per week, are less than is being paid by Poor Law Guardians all over Britain to those forced to accept relief from the poor rates . . . Those who condemn the seamen for [striking] actually ask us to believe in effect that no British mercantile marine is possible except on the basis of coolie conditions. But the P&O pays 12.5 per cent dividends all the same.

Continuing, the editorial said that Wilson and the *Daily Mail* in trotting out the 'Red Plot', the 'hidden hand of Moscow' and 'Russian gold', showed nothing but contempt for the British workers:

We take a better view of the British workers than that. May we remind their detractors on the editorial staffs of the New Zealand Capitalist press, who have rushed in to do Lord Inchcape's dirty work, that the British workers founded the trade union movement, and that for 150 years they were striking and fighting bad conditions before the Bolsheviks were ever heard of? And they would have continued to do so had Lenin and Trotsky and their comrades never appeared on this wretched planet.

The editorial then threw back the calumnies. They condemned those who were content to see their fellow countrymen living in poverty and who shrieked with hatred when they took risks with starvation to protect themselves. The seamen were to be congratulated for manifesting the spirit that would save our people.

The *NZ Worker* returned repeatedly to the defence of the seamen, to their right to strike and to the scandal of low wages. They also attacked the conservative press, the communist plot myth and the use of propaganda to break the strike. We quoted above the paper's rejection of lying reports that the strike was on the point of collapse. In the same issue (9 September) they returned to the right to strike. The British workers, they repeated, had fought and won the right to combine by strikes and agitation between 1800 and 1825 had fought the deportation of their leaders to Botany Bay and ever since, had been striking legally, 'to increase wages, reduce hours and improve conditions'.

Their right to combine and strike was won nearly a century before the Bolsheviks appeared in Russia, and it would have been exerted if the Soviet had never governed there. To say then that the seamen's strike is Bolshevism is either to betray ignorance or — cunning.

The paper supported the seamen 'because their action is a protest against the lie that industry must rest on a coolie basis' and because £2.5s a week was a sweated wage and a menace to the well-being of the people.

The Support Committees

Officials of the seamen's union in New Zealand were sympathetic, according to their official historian, but were 'chary of clashing with the official policy' of the British union.[6] Peter M Butler in Wellington and Fintan Patrick Walsh in Auckland stepped into the breach, persuaded local men not to scab and organized relief for the strikers. F P Walsh, a young seaman, formerly a member of the Communist Party, enhanced his reputation, leading to his assumption later of the leadership of the local seamen's union and the New Zealand labour movement.

In a letter of 2 December 1984, Butler wrote to the authors, describing his role during the strike. He was 24 years old, he said, when the British seamen just walked ashore in Wellington, Auckland, Dunedin, Napier and Lyttleton — 'protesters, without plans, and no recognized leaders, nor place of shelter'. In Wellington the Alliance of Labour organized financial aid for the men and Butler was asked by Jim Roberts, its secretary, to find accommodation for the men and raise finances from the unions. Butler had been a seaman. He wrote that in 1921:

When the first blast of post-war recession was felt, I had with other members of the Union Company's *Waikawa*, been jailed for a month in Sydney for refusing to sail the ship after all seamen's wages had been reduced. We had signed articles in New Zealand for a certain rate of wages, but on the voyage our wages were reduced; notwithstanding what we considered to be a legal binding bargain. Seamen in NZ also went out on strike, but we were licked.

Then came the strike of 1925. There were approximately 1,500 seamen out in New Zealand, 350 of whom were in Wellington. However no records were kept and there was little or no contact with the other ports. To underline the problems of the time, Butler commented, 'you have to realize that except for my then, inexpert assistance, there was no official interference or assistance'.

His position, he said, was that of 'liaison'. He kept contact with the strikers, organized and paid for lodgings and arranged concerts to augment funds.This was not difficult, because the obvious injustice of the employers, and the courage of the men, aroused 'unusual interest amongst the populace who expressed sympathy in every conceivable manner'. At first the task was relatively easy because the men slept on the ships, but this changed when they were not allowed aboard.

The support committee, according to Butler, 'had no office, equipment, correspondence or documents, nor minutes'. The men met at weekly meetings at the Alliance premises. These were concerned only with the progress of the strike. The police did not harass them and, when men were eventually charged, it was under British shipping laws that overrode local Acts.

In his letter Butler has underplayed his own role. During the strike he edited a strike bulletin, several copies of which have survived — and provide some indication of the mood of the time. Strike Bulletin No1 was both militant and unequivocal. Denying that there was a red plot the first article stated:

> ... the cause, the real cause of the industrial revolt is to be found in an analysis of the living and working conditions that our patriotic British shipowners, with the assistance of traitorous working class officials, are doing their damndest to force us to work under. In other words it is a manifestation of the class war, the fight of the capitalist employers against the workers of the world, and the fight must inevitably go on so long as capitalism lasts. It is up to the working class of the Empire to end it once and for all.

The articles are unsigned but it is quite likely that the writer of one piece in the second Bulletin was Butler. It took a courageous stand against colour discrimination and for that reason alone is worth quoting. The author claimed that the purpose of the capitalist system was to 'create surplus value' and increase profits. In so doing, they had little interest in whether the workers lived or died. The worker was struggling for higher wages because this paid for his subsistence — and because the subsistence level of the Lascar was so low ('so low as to be at the physical minimum required to restore the expended energy of the slave') his wages were kept down. This made the low wage a menace to higher wages, insufficient as they may be and a danger to all workers. The aim of higher paid workers should therefore be 'to remove these dangers, by close organization, by overcoming race prejudice and ignorance'. It is perhaps not insignificant that, as recorded in chapter four, one support committee had a black representative.

A further item that has survived from the activities of the support committees was a statement of accounts, kept by the Alliance of Labour, recording the receipts and payments of the 'Overseas Seamen's Fund'. It shows that £3,786 3s 1d was collected: half came from branches of the New Zealand Waterside Workers' Federation. This was a credit to the waterside workers, whose earnings had been greatly reduced because the number of ships being loaded or discharged had been affected by the strike.[7] Of the money collected all but £771 had been spent and the committee reported that in the long period of the strike, they were not aware of one seaman who went short of 'the necessaries of life'.[8] Of the balance, £500 was forwarded to the British Miners Federation. The remainder was kept to defray outstandin g expenditure.

'Victims of Wilson's Treachery'

On 9 September, the *NZ Worker* said that, because there was a complete hold-up of British ships in New Zealand waters, 'there was no need to report lengthily on this country'. But one week later developments focussed attention again on the British seamen who were being charged for being absent without leave and impeding the voyage of a vessel. On Monday, 14 September, eighty-six members of the crew of the *Arawa*, who had been charged and sentenced to six weeks imprisonment, marched to gaol, followed by some 500 sympathizers. The banners they carried included the messages:

WE PREFER JAIL TO STARVATION WAGES.

HEROES 1924, SLAVES 1925.

VICTIMS OF WILSON'S TREACHERY

Seamen in other ports were also sentenced. In Auckland the men were fined £215s and ordered to be put back on board their vessel. Iin Wellington the men were fined 10 days pay and imprisoned for 12 weeks and crew members of the *Horarata* at Christchurch (all ultimately imprisoned) were to appear in the court the coming week.[9]

The *NZ Worker* of 16 September condemned the imprisonment as 'exemplifying the victimization and brutal bullying' inflicted on workers by capitalism. It compared the praise bestowed on the seamen during the war and the treatment now meted out to men 'for the offence of refusing to starve for a pittance'. The paper was particularly incensed by editorials that 'gave them parting kicks with hoots and sneers' when they went to gaol:

Truly a sight for the gals! Pen-wielders, hacks of the wealthy, paid £1,000 a year or so, working diligently to convince the seamen that they are justly remunerated on £2 per week, and to project into the public mind the notion that the injustice is not in this despicable wage but in the protests of the workers against it. For cynicism and downright insolence this will take some beating...

.And such is capitalism. It cannot conceive of work as a service meriting a return in a full human life. Competition and inhuman 'economy' are its idols.

The Cost of the Strike to New Zealand

The *NZ Worker* of 7 October, reported an attack by H T Armstrong on the shipowners and also on the government for its craven attitude towards them. He started his address on the point at which the strike hit the country the hardest: its dependence on world trade. The blockage affected every person in the country, he said, and not least the worker, who was dependent on the continued production of goods for export.

Armstrong defended the seamen and attacked Wilson for accepting the cut in wages. Then he proceeded to state the case that had been publicized prominently in the socialist press of Britain, Australia and South Africa. The seamen worked for £9 a month, but were on unemployment relief when in port, and on this their families had to subsist. This was iniquitous he proclaimed, not only because the seamen had rendered such service to the Empire during the last war, but also because the shipowners had made such huge profits then, and continued to profit from the trade they plied since. He quoted the well known passage from the book by the British Labour MP Christopher Addison:[10]

> I often used to say to them, and I think still that if the public could have been provided with an account of the disposition and earnings of the ships in those times of national peril, some owners might have found an end on the nearest lamp-post, and there would have been some rough justice in it.

These companies, he declared, were prepared to have their ships built in Germany at the expense of British ship builders, and were now prepared to cut the seamen's wages until their families were down to the poverty line. Then throwing out a challenge to the government he asked whether they stood: 'with Lord Inchcape and the other profiteers . . . men who are concerned with nothing but profits . . . or with the British seamen who have rendered such splendid service to the Empire . . .? It was a rhetorical question, the answer to which, from a Tory government, was obvious.

Nonetheless the impact of the strike on the local economy was of growing concern to the government. Sir James Parr, New Zealand's Minister of Justice, was quoted as saying:

> In Auckland alone nine [sixteen actually] overseas ships were held up by the seamen's strike. New Zealand was never faced with a more serious situation. The inward and outward cargoes involved were over £2,750,000 in value. Probably three quarters of the cargo were primary products destined for England, while inward merchandise was urgently required by the importers and the public. He estimated that New Zealand produce and meat to the value of £4,500,000 was held up. If the strike continued into the summer, our exports, 96 per cent of which are primary products would not be forwarded, and the country would lose £50,000,000 in the year. The strike had got the whole community by the throat, and a continuance would mean the closing down of every industry, office and business in New Zealand.[11]

He concluded: 'The Government realized the gravity of the situation, and could not stand by and see the country ruined'.

At the end of September Gordon Coates, the Prime Minister, said he hoped to mediate and end the strike. If however such negotiations were protracted or failed the government was bound to take steps, 'to ensure that overseas ships could move from port to port, that cargo could be handled, and that when loaded, vessels could proceed to sea'.[12] He then invited Butler, through the Marine Superintendent, to meet and discuss the situation. In reply, Butler said that he had no mandate, and that men should be released from prison so that he could consult with them. Thirty men were released and met in conference on 5–6 October, with Butler in attendance and Coates in the chair.[13] The men then met with the employer's agents on the 6th. There they demanded the immediate release of imprisoned men with a £1 a day compensation for all sentences served, the payment of full wage and allotment for dependents since the strike began, payment for board and lodgings incurred by strikers while ashore, remission of all fines, penalties, and law costs, cancellation of all log book entries, and no prosecutions of strikers and no victimization. Also, new articles to be signed at the rates prior to July.[14]

The employers, said Butler, demanded an immediate return to work under existing articles, no wages for the period of the strike, no remission of fines, no prosecution if the men returned immediately, with clean discharges dependent on behaviour on the return journey; and a partial payment of family allotments.[15] This was rejected by the seamen.

Coates' response was to claim that 'the only thing remaining to be done was promptly to get the New Zealand produce away and to protect those who would undertake the work'.[16] This was a scab's charter and, under police protection crews were recruited, partly from the non-seafaring public and from among strikers anxious to return home. By 7 October the *Ruahine* had a full complement, and with a cargo worth £800,000 on board sailed from Auckland. On the 12th the *Arawa* was manned and sailed and there were reports of 'considerable free labour' being available at the docks.[17]

From 10 October onwards there were reports in the press of clashes between seamen and scab labour. However, the situation was fluid as shown in the case of the *Hororata*. Its crew of twenty five was released early from gaol on condition that they returned immediately to their ship and took up duties. Yet, when the ship prepared to sail, crew members claimed that they found a shortage of hands both on deck and among the firemen. They protested that it was against the law to sail under these conditions and they left the ship by boarding the tugs. Immediately rearrested, they were sentenced to prison again.[18]

On some ships there was a game of 'musical chairs'. When 'free labour' was employed to replace strikers on the *Dorset* in Wellington nineteen of the existing crew left the ship. A second batch of scabs was brought in from Taranaki farms and the ship moved out of anchorage, there to await further developments. What happened next appears in a 'Report of the Secretary of the Nev Zealand Waterside Workers' Federation, 1925':

> Early in September the Alliance of Labour asked the seamen to hand their dispute to them. We could see at that time that the British shipping trust were (*sic*) determined to defeat the semen at all cost. The men, however, refused to do this, and it was not until after the 21st October that they handed over their dispute to the New Zealand Alliance of Labour.
>
> That organization fully considered the issue and it was unanimously agreed to advise the men to return to their ships.[19]

With the ships being manned, the Alliance intervened to advise the men to return to work. Walsh and Butler agreed with them. The decision was placed before seamen in Wellington and Auckland (at least) and appears to have been accepted.[20] The strike was called off in New Zealand on 29 October. However, as the paper said, there were still some 400 men stranded in New Zealand — the rest having been reinstated. Consequently, Alliance representatives saw Coates on 10 November and requested that: shipowners (and in particular the Shaw Savil Company) be compelled to reinstate all the men with those for whom no berths were available being repatriated or jobs found for them in New Zealand and that all men in jail be released. The outcome of the meeting was unclear, Coates giving them 'a Yes/No answer'.[21] All that could be reported was that some men had since been released from prison.

Some seamen maintained the strike beyond the end of October. One month later, on 1 December the *NZ Transport Worker* reported that some 5,000 men were still out in Australia, 2,000 in South Africa and (an unreported number) in New Zealand. Although sailing from Great Britain had become more regular during the past week, the situation was so serious that press reports intimated that shipowners were considering curtailing sailing to the three Dominions. This was the inevitable consequence of a lack of central directives and the fragmentation of the seamen's organization over the five continents. Although the owners maintained a world-wide combine, the men were organized locally and the secretary of New Zealand Waterside Workers was quite certain, 'that if the transport workers in Australasia, South Africa and those of Great Britain [were] affiliated, the seamen's strike would not have ended the way it [had] done'.[22]

9

THE STRIKE GRINDS DOWN

'The Scab on the Ocean Wave'

The TUC tried in July and August to amlgamate the NSFU and AMWU. Havelock Wilson agreed, but the move was rejected by the AMWU on the grounds that Wilson would swallow the smaller union and exclude its leading members. The TUC tried bribery. It suggested in August that Shinwell, Lewis, Cannon and McKinlay be paid £1,000 each (as compensation for loss of office), provided they stayed out of future seamen's affairs. This was rejected by the four men and made public by Shinwell at the Trades Union Congress conference on 8 September 1925.

In the run up to the conference the *Daily Record and Mail* commented on the TUC's role in the strike. Its weekly 'London Letter' on 2 September said that Walter Citrine, TUC assistant secretary, was questioned about its failure to support the NSFU 'in its fight for the sanctity of a properly arrived at agreement'. Citrine said that the matter would be discussed at the next meeting and he would not answer the question that followed: 'Was the AMWU exploiting the situation for the purpose of injuring Wilson's union?' The answer, said the columnist was obvious and he continued:

> Yet the [NSFU] has been left to fight single-handed, with its rival hanging on to its flank, counselling the men to repudiate their own leaders and their own word. If ever there was a clear cut case for immediate support from the parent body, here is one ...

Two days later Shinwell denied that he would be asking the TUC for assistance in the strike. It was not customary, he said, to make such application in the first few days of a conflict — ignoring the fact that the strike had been in progress in London for over three weeks.[1] On Friday night (4 September) Shinwell altered course. He told a meeting in Poplar Town Hall that he would represent the AMWU at the conference and would defend the strikers and the union against any attacks. He said that he asked the TUC, if there was any doubt about it, to stand aside, express no opinion, and leave the men to fight it out with the Shipping Federation and the NSFU. Then he added:

> But I know my trade union friends better than that. I know the miners too well to believe that they are going to let the seamen down, and I believe they will assist the seamen, as they expected the seamen to assist them in their own day of toil and tribulation. *If that is not done, and if the seamen are left without any friends or support on the part of the trade union movement, then it will be an end to all talk about fighting the employers in their attempts to reduce wages.*[2]

Although he added that he believed the seamen could win if they only stood firm, his prediction would stand as a warning that the trade union movement could only ignore at its peril. If the strike were lost the leadership of Havelock Wilson would be entrenched and there would be no support from the seamen's union for any workers in struggle.

That evening there had been significant support for the strike in Southampton: Delegates of practically the whole trade union movement in Southampton and district attended a special meeting ... of the Trades and Labour Council, which passed a resolution giving full support to the strikers and pledging themselves to do all in their power to prosecute the strike to a successful issue. Further, the meeting called upon the Trades Union Congress to take steps to bring about a successful settlement.[3]

Havelock Wilson and Joseph Cotter were safely aboard the *Mauretania* however, on a trip that took them to Canada and New York. When the conference opened, supporters of both the NMM and the AMWU were present. Nine NSFU members from Hull lobbied the opening session with posters declaring: 'No PC5! Down with Havelock Wilson and the Shipping Federation!'

The demonstrators told reporters that they 'would like to know what Havelock Wilson was doing in Canada when the TUC conference is in Scarborough'. Leaders of the NSFU were greeted with shouts of 'Traitor'. The Central Strike Committee deputation were refused a hearing and were forced (reluctantly, they said) to distribute a statement:

This treacherous betrayer of the seamen, Mr Havelock Wilson has also betrayed the whole trade union movement. Had the officials of the [NSFU] acted as they ought to have done ... they would have consulted the General Council and Allied Unions before accepting reductions, and we feel certain that no reductions would have taken place had they sought the co-operation of the Trade Union Movement as the miners did.[4]

The TUC would not allow discussion of an unofficial strike and Shinwell could only raise the issue tangentially during discussion on the failure of the amalgamation talks. He was not allowed to talk about the strike, said a member of the General Purposes Committee, because they did not want the Congress turned into a 'bear garden'.

The NSFU delegates were accepted as the spokesmen of the seamen even though they stood aloof from discussions of the strike, both before and at the conference.: those claiming to speak for the strikers receiving no support then or through the period of the strike. On the contrary, unions with men working on the seafront insisted that their members continue work, even if this effectively involved strike breaking.[6] Finally, after a complaint from delegate James Sexton MP, a placard on the platform with the words *The Scab on the Ocean Wave* was removed from the hall because 'it was libellous upon the organizations affiliated to this congress'.

The NMM, tied to Lazovsky and the Red International of Labour Unions, was unable to press the semen's claim effectively inside the TUC. Its strategy was directed to upholding the agreement of the TUC and the Soviet trade unions in a so-called United Front. Because of this they were reluctant to criticise, but dared not stay silent. Thus they pleaded:

> The time has come for the General Council of the TUC to take up the seamen's case. If the seamen are defeated the first breach will be made in the Workers' United Front, and the Boss class will be encouraged to press forward its offensive.[7]

The Workers United Front was a chimera. But the deeper implication of the statement was correct. If the seamen's strike was defeated the offensive against the unions would be 'pressed forward'. Shinwell had also seen the danger to the unions in the event of a defeat of the strike, but the warnings seemed to go unnoticed.

A final attempt to involve the TUC in the seamen's strike failed. A deputation from the Southampton Emergency Shipyard Workers' Committee visited Fred Bramley, secretary of the TUC in London, because they were unwilling to staff ships worked by scabs. A mass meeting of 2,000 shipyard workers also called for a boycott of ships that had used scab labour. The Executive Committees of all the unions concerned were requested to sanction a withdrawal of labour and secure the support of the TUC for an early and satisfactory settlement.[8] In a parallel move seventeen unions representing every section of shipyard workers in Southampton were invited by the Plumbers' Society to an emergency conference to discuss the situation in the yard.

Before it could convene, the engineering and shipbuilding unions informed their members in Southampton that no action to support the seamen could be countenanced. Many of the men were represented on the NMB, it was said, and any unauthorized action would be a distinct breach of honour. Some officials were summoned by their Executives to explain their involvement in the unofficial movements and ordered to withdraw 'sympathetic pledges or offers of support which could not be redeemed'.[9] Only six small craft unions attended the Plumbers' Society's conference and in Southampton the only support available was from the local trades council, which had pledged to assist the seamen earlier in the month.[10] The TUC position was restated by Bramley: 'it could not ... intervene in a dispute which was not even recognized by the men's own executives'.[11]

Poverty and the Board of Guardians

Early in the strike the seamen were deemed not to be at work and the employers stopped the portion of the wages (or allotment) that was paid at intervals during the voyage. This had an immediate affect on the seamen's families. They had barely survived under the old rate of pay and the August wage cut had reduced them to the barest subsistence. The families had little or no savings and stopping the pay to wives was intended to bring pressure to bear on the men abroad. Some families were fortunate in winning the sympathy particularly of the women in the communities around the docks and this must have helped alleviate some of the very worst hardship. But there was less understanding from women outside the seafaring communities. Some (including several former militant suffragettes) condemned all strike action and criticized the seamen for neglecting their wives.

There were sharply contrasting letters in the press from women who supported or opposed strike action, the latter referring to the 'red menace', the plight of the shipowners, and so on. A woman who signed herself 'A Wife and Mother' wrote:

A great number of married men go to sea, they allot their wives 30s per week, and pay off with a little over a pound after an 18 days' run. That, along with the few shillings shore pay, has to see the wife and children through a week, until she is entitled to draw her first allotment, after the sailing of the ship.

Also the wife has some six to eight weeks unemployment to look forward to each winter, and in the case of the *Majestic* in the early part of this year — four months, plus 10 days in August . . .

I do not hold with strikes, or with the men who organize them, but I do respect the English workman for putting up a fight to gain a living wage for those dependent on him.[12]

But fight as they did, the men achieved little. As well as the combined might of the shipowners, they faced authorities who were on the offensive and refused them relief. On 3 September about 1,000 seamen in Liverpool who had applied for the dole were given notice that their benefits were suspended for six weeks, because they had not accepted other 'suitable employment'.[13] A mass meeting of seamen was called where the men were informed by the local Board of Guardians that it was illegal to pay out-door relief to persons on strike. This was followed on the Sunday by a procession of about 500 men through the south end of the city. A deputation met with the Deputy Chairman and the Master of the Board of Guardians to discuss the question of relief but was told that each case would be discussed on its merits. By mid-September about 1,100 seamen had applied to the Board but most were refused payment even though many had been on relief before the strike began. However they were told their wives and children could apply and all genuine cases of distress would be relieved.

On 14 September, 300 men, led by M E Boggin the local strike leader, marched behind a band singing *We are the Boys of the Bulldog Breed* and demanded out-door relief from the Board of Guardians. In an obvious delaying tactic the men were told to apply individually and in due course most were found to be entitled to some payments.[14]

The procession became a daily feature in Liverpool and the seamen were joined by their wives, some carrying children, and by the unemployed. This continued through September until marches were banned by the police because they 'were leading to disorder'. That is, there were reports that 'a procession of strikers with red banners and drums, augmented by 100 women bag makers who had taken the day off to show their sympathy with the strikers' had assaulted four firemen seen leaving the White Star liner, the *Adriatic*. Also, women had shouted 'A scab lives there' when passing certain houses to urge the crowd to break the windows as it passed.[15] While AMWU leaders favoured an end to these daily demonstrations, members of the strike committee although angry but still announced that they were all joining the AMWU. Boggin explained:

... we did not join the AMWU in the first instance because we had the alternative of joining the Transport Workers ... But when the Trade Unions ordered their men to remain at work in the 'scab' ships *Doric* and *Adriatic*, we
came to the conclusion that Mr [Ernest] Bevin (General Secretary) was in
the same category as Havelock Wilson.[16]

Conditions in other towns were equally bad and, in an endeavour to break the
strike, unemployed seamen who could not produce a NSFU card could not get unemployment benefit.[17] In Southampton, approximately 1,400 men were on strike
and many families had men on strike abroad. There was some relief for members
of the AMWU when 15s strike pay became available on Friday 11 September. For
non-members, money was raised through donations and street collections. However, it was estimated that about 3–400 families were in dire distress and in need of
Poor Law help after allotments were stopped.[18] Relief for these families was given
in kind only – recipients receiving the bare necessities of life from bakers and
grocers.[19]

If there were demonstrations outside Liverpool they were not reported in the
press. Many seamen accepted berths in desperation and, as frustration grew,
demonstrations grew rowdier or strikers turned to violence, and there was a per-
ceptible increase in the number of cases brought to court. Windows of the NSFU
offices were smashed[20] and scabs were attacked in many ports. One report stated:

It appears that non-strikers on their way to the docks were stopped by a party
of seamen strikers and the resultant encounter ended in blows. The collision
caused excitement amongst the people of the neighbourhood and the
strikers' pickets from various points in Canute Rd rushed to the scene. An estimated crowd of 200 gathered, including many women. Information was
given to the police and a strong contingent of the force arrived to deal with
the trouble, which was tempestuous while it lasted, but had almost subsided
when the police arrived and dispersed the crowd.[21]

Some incidents involved racial attacks. One report said:

feeling among unemployed white seamen against black labour, which has
been very strong at Swansea for some weeks past, culminated this morning in
a disturbance at the docks ...[22]

Knives and other weapons were brandished, but the police intervened and
separated the men.There is no indications of how the issue was finally
resolved.

The Men Go Back

Despite the large number of men on strike in the ports, blackleg crews were
recruited and the ships kept sailing. The media regaled the public with the
victories scored by the giant liners as they came into port, took on passengers
and eventually sailed – with each departure hailed as a major victory. This
was the era in which the newsreel was coming into its own, and the press
seemed to be in daily competition with the motion pictures in its eagerness to
dramatize the 'battle' in the ports. It is not easy at this remove to separate

press sensationalism from the reality of the August and September days of 1925. As the big ships prepared, particularly for the cross-Atlantic sailings, all news was focused on their arrivals and departures. Would the *Majestic* sail? Would there be a crew? Would the strikers be stopped? Columns of ink were spilt in telling the story of the battle between the shipping lines and the 'reds'.

When the *Majestic* did sail at the beginning of September, the press was jubilant and announced that the strikers had been defeated. It was now a matter of hours, or at most a day, before the strike would collapse. Perhaps the battle of words reflected what was happening in Southampton, London, Liverpool or Hull — or perhaps this was also part of the war of attrition in which the aim was to break the morale of the strikers. Our reading of events indicates that the fight was real, and all the resources available to the owners were used to get ships to sea. This could be done, however difficult, if there was no effective force at the journey's end to support any dissident crewmen. It was on the journey out to Australasia or South Africa that initial sailings could not be repeated because the ships just did not return. In British ports the ships had sailed in late August with blackleg crews, and at the New York end of the run police stood by to stop any demonstrations against the seamen.

On 11 September the *Evening News* reported that some 200 American 'reds' reinforced by longshoremen were at the pier in New York to jeer at the *Majestic* as it arrived. The demonstration was broken up by police. The US unions gave no support to the strike and ultimately, when the strike was over, the NSFU received a cable stating:

> The great American Federation of Labour Convention, representing the whole of organized labour of America, at Atlantic City, unanimously adopted a resolution congratulating the officers and members of the National Sailors' and Fireman's Union of Great Britain on their firm stand against the Reds and destructionists.[23]

The pickets tried to intercept the strike breakers but, as the weeks dragged on and families grew hungrier, only the most determined continued the fight. On 2 October both the *Daily Herald*, and the *Weekly Worker* reported that a meeting attended by representatives from all the ports (and including members of the AMWU) had decided to fight on with renewed vigour. However, in October the shipping agents abroad were getting the ships turned round, and this was a sign that the strike was crumbling.

On 8 October the first mail, specie, passengers and cargo, arrived in Southampton from the Cape, after a break of over a month. The *Arundle Castle* carried 1,000 bags of mail, gold worth £800,000, 24,000 boxes of oranges and 160 passengers. Its crew included a clergyman, an opera singer and some undergraduates coming to British colleges who thought it was 'a huge joke' to come over as members of the crew. With no accepted central authority to call off the strike, the end came when men in Durban decided to return to work. They consulted the AMWU first and then agreed to sail, the minority accepting the decision 'under protest'.[24] The AMWU called a meeting of representatives from the main ports (London excepted) and after a ballot it was decided to end the strike in Great

Britain although, it was added, in some ports the majority of men still said that they were opposed to the wage cut. In a statement announcing the decision the AMWU added:

> ... the seamen's protest was necessary and justified, particularly in view of the men not being consulted about the wage reduction, and resolves that in all the circumstances it is now advisable to bring the dispute to an end, but only on the understanding that steps be taken to reorganize the National Maritime Board so as to secure effective representation of all seamen's unions, and the right of qualified seamen to employment without PC5 or any other interference with the right to enrol in any seamen's organization they desire.

> In the event of these decisions not being complied with a national conference of all organizations of seamen be immediately called with a view to action being taken to enforce the claims.[25]

The ending of the strike did not alter the position of the men on shore. There were few berths available either because the ships were away or because returning crews (including those who had opposed the strike) were retained by the ships' masters. The Central Strike Committee, secure only in London, nonetheless disputed the right of the AMWU to call off the strike, maintaining that feeling in Britain was solid for continuing the fight. Claiming that the seamen had been betrayed by both the NSFU and the AMWU, the CSC added that at a mass meeting in London the men had voted for the creation of a seamen's section of the Transport and General Workers Union and had approached the secretary to put this into effect.[26]

But this was the end of the road. A mass meeting in London of 1,500 seamen decided, by a majority of one vote it was said, to end the strike. The decision was regretted, said the Committee, particularly as the men in Australia were 'fighting with all possible vigour' and a cable from Walsh said they were determined to carry on the struggle. The CSC, it was said, would be maintained to conduct relief work among the seamen and their families and the NMM would now organize seamen's groups in every port in the British isles.[27]

The Wireless Operators

The strike ended raggedly in South Africa and was not yet over in Australia — but the traffic was moving, even if delayed. But even when the firemen and deckhands had all returned the ships in the Pacific Ocean faced one last protest from the wireless operators, a small but nonetheless important group To place this last action in context it is necessary to glance back briefly. There were another thirteen smaller organizations, some national, the others local, that catered for seafarers.[28] One of these organizations, the Association of Wireless and Cable Telegraphists (AWCT), started as a wireless operators union in 1912 with forty–five members. In 1921 the AWCT had incorporated the Cable Telegraph Operators' Association, and since then it had represented approximately 4,500 members. The union always faced implacable opposition from their employers, Marconi International Marine Communication, Siemens Brothers, and Radio Communication Co. The shipowners resisted the extension of radio to cargo vessels until legislation in 1919 required a radio operator in cargo ships over 1,600 tons. Ships carrying over 200 persons needed three operators, one with at least three years' experience. When operators came out on strike, in June 1920 and April 1922, shipowners declared that wireless was not essential and the Board of Trade allowed ships to sail either with untrained operators or with none at all. In 1925 the one pound cut in salary was to have been phased in to cover the wireless operators as well but the measure was postponed while the main body of men were on strike. When the crews returned to work the shipowners announced that they were putting into effect the cuts of 5s per week on wireless operators. This led to the calling of a strike from 28 November. There had been little or no support for the seamen from these officers[29] — and now they were isolated. The British Board of Trade intervened and waived the regulations requiring each ship to carry three operators and on 24 December the affected ships sailed with scab labour. Thus ended the last phase of the strike of 1925.

The Price They Paid

On 14 November the *Times* carried a Reuter dispatch from Australia stating that the lines there had lost an estimated £2,000,000 in freights alone as a result of the strike. This, said the writer, was an impressive figure but could not be 'a true measure of the total losses'. To the figure of two million pounds had to be added the cost of maintaining the vessels, idle for months. There were port charges and pay and food for the loyal staff and there were permanent losses of freight to foreign companies. Also, now that services had resumed, the ships would have to depart at regular intervals so that the usual rotation of crafts be secured for the future. This would involve idling in port for many more months. The cost of all this, said the *Times* writer, was incalculable. Also, it was not possible to calculate the cost to producers of perishable commodities that had been wasted because there was no transport available. In like fashion the losses to New Zealand and South Africa, and in Great Britain were colossal. At a much earlier date the high cost of the strike had been noted on both sides of the class line. For example, on 23 September, the *Australian Worker* had said

> So wealthy is the Shipping Combine that it doesn't seem to care how much the breaking of the strike costs. Whatever the expenditure involved, the men must be ground beneath the iron heel of mastership.
>
> Already in Australia, the laying up of the ships, in harbour charges alone, has cost the owners as much as would have paid the men the disputed pound a month for ten years. And when to that amount is added the loss in freights and fares — an incalculable sum — it is not too much to say that what the Combine has lost in this country alone exceeds what it would gain in many years from the whole British service by the enforcement of the proposed reduction in wages.

Yet it is prepared to go even further than that. Cabled advices state that the shipowners contemplate stopping all sailings for Australia until the men are starved into surrender.

The owners had said it all in the columns of *Fairplay*. On 10 September they claimed that the strike was 'the first fruits of the Government's poltroonery in the matter of the coal miner's dispute'. The government had 'paid blackmail' and this had given the communists their opportunity. If the authorities had stood firm, as indeed the shipowners had, the upheaval could have been averted.

The *Australian Worker*, of 23 September had also said:

the whole thing owes its genesis to the passionate desire of International Capitalism to smash the power of the Unions, and through them the political Labour Movement, because the Unions and the Labour Movement stand in the way of the establishment of a Capitalist Dictatorship extending to all parts of the globe.

Read at this remove it sounds fantastical. Yet, in the spirit of the time, with Mussolini now entrenched in Rome and the corporate state appearing to grow through Europe, this was a fearful prospect for the labour movement. The paper continued, noting that:

The Shipping combine is an international body ... There is hardly a nation it does not exploit ... [and in this] Bruce ... is the puppet of a foreign combine attempting to smash down the conditions of the workers ...

For the working class this was a grim warning that seemed all too real after the events of the past three months. Yet the trade union movement in Great Britain had seen nothing and heard nothing. Nor had it said anything. Leading trade unionists either turned their backs on the seamen or pleaded tamely that they could not give support to an unofficial strike. They ignored the warnings of Shinwell and others, that a defeat for the seamen would be disastrous for the trade union movement, avoided a confrontation with Havelock Wilson and the NSFU and watched while the militant action of the seamen was smashed.

Must we invoke the scriptures and say of them: 'They knew not what they were doing'? And if we did, could we ask for forgiveness?

10

STRIKE AGAINST THE TIDE

On Not Wanting a Bear Garden

The seamen's strike of 1925 appears to have been relegated to the footnotes of labour history, at the time it dominated the main pages of newspapers in three continents. And then silence.[1] This omission, as we said in the preface is inexplicable.

In Great Britain the strike was overshadowed by the dispute in the coalfields and bodies like the Communist Party of Great Britain warned constantly of the threatened assault on the working class movement, linking the government's offensive with the European-wide attacks on the labour movement. The fascist movement in Mussolini's Italy was a source of concern to the left and, although there was little theorising about such movements at the time, the possibility of their appearing in Britain seemed ominous. Above all else, this was a period preceding the general strike and everyone knew that conflict had only been delayed on 31 July. It might have been only coincidental that the wage cut in the merchant marine was agreed a few days after employers served notice of cuts on the coal mines. Yet it looks remarkably like a provocation. Was this perhaps the testing of a vital work force in which the government could stand aloof and allow the shipowners and the National Seamen and Fireman's Union to put their workers in their place?

In the absence of any evidence that might be fanciful. Yet we can only ask why the trade union leaders did not heed the warning of Shinwell that the two events were connected. When the TUC met in Conference there was no discussion on this issue. The seamen's pickets were ignored, the strikers' poster (*The Scab on the Ocean Wave*) was removed from the platform, the absence of Wilson was not remarked upon by the conference leaders and all that the Standing Committee of the TUC could say was that it did *'not want a bear garden'*!

The strike went against the tide of events with every factor loaded against it succeeding. It was a strike against one of the most powerful combines in the world, able to sit out any work stoppage and determined to smash opposition and it was a strike against the trade union that was nominally the protector of the seamen's interests. Furthermore, it was a strike that the TUC was determined to ignore. The seamen were also unfortunate in having supporters who used the struggle to advance their own objectives, at least in Great Britain. The splinter union, the Amalgamated Marine Workers Union, was as much interested in using the strike to advance their organization as they were in advancing the interests of the seafarers and the Central Strike Committee always had one eye on the requirements of the

Anglo-Russian committee and on the objectives of the Red International of Labour Unions.

It was also a period in which the strains in the labour movement turned the attention of many persons in other directions. Other events had to be addressed and they seemed more important at the time than the plight of seamen, many of them thousands of miles away. When the strike ultimately came to a ragged end attention was also diverted elsewhere. On 14 October police raided the headquarters of the Communist Party, the Young Communist League, the National Minority Movement and the party's press and the offices or private homes of members of the CPGB. Leading members of the CPGB were charged with uttering seditious libel and inciting persons to commit breaches of the Incitement to Mutiny Act of 1797.[2] There was no mention of the seamen's strike in the charges and the activities of the NMM were never broached. Was there really no connection, and was the date of the raids, so soon after the ending of the strike in London, a coincidence? We do not know, and there are no documents to link the events. We have looked in vain, in publications of the CPGB, to check for connections, only to find that even its official historian makes no mention of the one strike in which the NMM played so prominent a role.[3]

If later commentators overlooked the strike, those immediately affected spoke about, or wrote about its impact: the seamen and their wives, the union leaders and labour politicians (more particularly in the Dominions), the shipowners and those who actively opposed the strike in the NSFU and the financial columnists. We have already discussed the impact of the strike on the economies of Australia, South Africa and New Zealand. In Britain, the closing of the shipping lines led to increased prices for food — in particular meat, dairy products, cattle food, and fruit.[4] British exports, presumably, fared better: some 60 per cent of cargo having been shipped from Britain, even before the strike, in vessels under foreign flags.[5] Yet the tying up or delaying of even 40 per cent of the country's exports must have been felt when British exports were declining.

Important as the economic factors were, they were secondary to the government in its total strategy: the smashing of trade union resistance. On 25 September the press carried reports on the Organization for the Maintenance of Supplies (OMS), that was already 'organizing those citizens who would be prepared to volunteer to maintain supplies and vital services in the event of a general strike'.[6] The organization claimed initially that it was independent and non-political but on 1 October a letter in the *Times* from the Home Secretary stated that the OMS had been formed with the knowledge and approval of the government.

With a dozen leading communists facing charges and concern rising about government plans for coming industrial strife, the priority accorded the seamen through August and September receded. Amidst all the recrimination that followed defeat, the problems of the merchant marine were relegated to the back pages. But the problems did not go away and, particularly in London, there were new attempts by seafarers to break away from the NSFU. On 30 October 1925 the *Workers Weekly* called on seamen to stay in the NSFU. Saying that there was 'a feeling of utter disgust towards the NSFU and the AMWU' the paper noted that there was a tendency to leave these unions, join other unions or form a new body. The paper also reported a meeting of transport workers in which Hardy, the NMM member assigned to the seamen's section, was subjected to heckling by members of the National Amalgamated Union of Stevedores, Lightermen, Watermen and Dockers, generally known as the Blue Union. Hardy opposed entry to this small union, which was local and not affiliated to the TUC. The NMM urged the men to stay in the NSFU until the General Council of the TUC sanctioned the formation of a seamen's section of the Transport and General Workers' Union (TGWU). However, the TGWU did not form a seamen's section, the Blue Union did not provide the facilities the seamen needed. With no effective organization in London the NMM lost all authority.[7] On 6 November the AMWU, in a letter to the Shipping Federation, tried again to break the PC5 barrier requesting a meeting to discuss the NMB and the engaging of crews. The reply from the Executive Council on 20 November was curt and negative. It would not meet the AMWU,

... having regard to the recent action of your Executive in supporting the Communist attack on British shipping, and in affording countenance and encouragement to mutinous conduct on the part of seamen in Colonial ports .

The Executive Council also decided to tighten relations with the NSFU and see that decisions of the NMB were properly carried out. Havelock Wilson had intimated that 'his union should enter into a bond in a large sum of money as a guarantee' that all future agreements would be carried out. The Federation executive was divided but decided that this might only cause trouble 'because his union was not now very much in favour'. The Federation continued to support the NSFU.

With the aid of the employers, Wilson was bound to destroy the rival union — and the process was speeded when Booth of the AMWU went over to the NSFU. Booth declared that the amalgamation of the BSU and the Cooks and Stewards Union in 1921 was invalid because the poll had been less than the legally required 50 per cent. A High Court injunction stopped the AMWU from using the funds or property of the Cooks and Stewards Union. The result was disastrous. The AMWU funds were all tied up and there was no money even to disentangle the assets. Within six months, membership declined drastically, the union folded up and Wilson reigned supreme.

But before the AMWU was disposed of, the NSFU was involved in the most shameful of Wilson's escapades. When the General Council of the TUC instructed workers to take part in the General Strike, the NSFU was the only union that refused to participate. Wilson argued that strike action needed the consent of the workers and that a two-third majority on a ballot was required. He also said the union could not justify the breaking of their agreement with the shipowners.[8]

A minority of seamen came out with the AMWU, and they were joined unofficially by members of the NSFU in London, on Merseyside and Tyneside. Wilson sacked the officials of the offending branches and sought a High Court injunction stopping members from coming out on strike.[9] At the hearing Wilson also argued that the General Strike was contrary to the law. After a brief hearing Mr Justice Astbury granted an injunction restraining officials of the Tower Hill branch from calling out mermbers in support of the strike. He went further and stated that no trade dispute had been shown to exist between any of the unions and the employers except in the case of the coal miners. Consequently the orders of the TUC to the unions was unlawful.. There is no indication that the TUC took any steps at this stage to discipline Wilson.

Tthro ugh the nine days of the strike the NSFU assisted the Shipping Federation in getting scabs onto any strike-bound ships.Seamen dispirited after the defeat of 1925 and faced with the court decision had little option but to man the ships and bring coal into Britain or face dismissal. The officials of the International Transport Workers Federation proteste, saying that they could hardly call on workers in Europe not to load coal or prevent seamen signing on in British ships, when British seamen continued to work.[10]

Subsequently Wilson supported the Miners Industrial (or Spencer) Union in Nottinghamshire and offered them a loan of £10,000. The new union was given the use of NSFU officials and cars and issued the breakaway MIU journal from the seamen's union headquarters. It was this that finally led to the expulsion of the NSFU from the TUC. Wilson was neither intimidated nor deflected from his course and in October he announced the establishment of the Industrial Peace Union.[11]

In a reversal of policy Tom Walsh made his peace in 1926 with Wilson and became a firm ally of the NSFU. Details of what occurred are not clear but the CPA paper, the *Weekly Worker*, of 24 and 31 March 1926 claimed that Walsh, tiring of the fight, and afraid of losing his position to Johnson, contacted Wilson and the NSFU. Thereafter he redrafted the rules of the Australian seamen's union to give himself dictatorial powers (in line with the NSFU constitution). By 1928 Walsh and his wife Adela Pankhurst (sister of the famous suffragette), had moved to the far right. They supported the Industrial Peace Union and were protagonists of the White Australia policy. Havelock Wilson had won yet another battle. Or perhaps it was the nature of trade unionism and the power that fell into the hands of the trade union bosses that led to this chameleon change in Walsh. It was only after a bitter internal fight that Johnson replaced him as leader of the Australian seamen and the *status quo ante* was restored. Or so it seemed, until Johnson was in turn removed from office after being accused by members of the union's executive of doing precisely what Walsh had done a few years back.

There can be no ending to an event that sent such ripples, if not shock waves, across the Empire. But there was one terminal point in the saga: Havelock Wilson, an ill man in the last years of his life, died in 1929. To the very end he was able to conceal events surrounding his personal life. The second volume of his autobiography, which would have covered the period of our essay, never appeared. He claimed that the manuscript had been sent to the US but it has never been seen. There is an even bigger mystery over his will, which disclosed that he had left under £700. That has as little credibility as most other events in his life. What happened to the rest of his assets is unknown. One legacy he did leave, and that is summarised in the statement printed under the photo of Havelock Wilson, CH, CBE. Appearing in the *Seaman* of 5 January 1929, the journal of the union named since 1925, the

National Union of Seamen. The words are from the pen of Lord Inchcape, the man who gained most from the defeat of the British seamen. He said that:

> There is no man who has done more for what we are all striving for, and which the Government is striving for, and that is Peace in Industry for our beloved country, than Mr Havelock Wilson.

Havelock Wilson was dying when these words were written. They stand as an epitaph, written from the point of view of the employers and apparently endorsed by those who controlled the union. It is doubtful whether many of the 140,000 seamen in the British merchant marine would have agreed.

REFERENCES

Introduction, pp 1–6

1. The rank and file movement led by the British Communist Party and affiliated to the Red International of Labour Unions (Profintern).
2. Leaders of the AMWU were alone in recognizing it as a prelude to the coming struggle: the defeat of the seamen presaged the coming defeat of the entire trade union movement in 1926.
3. *Westralian Worker*, 2 October. All newspapers, unless otherwise mentioned are for 1925.
4 *Ibid*, 6 November.
5 *Workers Weekly*, 28 August.
6. See Olssen. The quotations from his article refer to conditions on New Zealand ships. Conditions on other ships were no different.

Background to a Strike, pp 7–12

1. Editorial, Vol 4, No 9, September.
2. Calhoun, pp 172–73; Farman, pp 38–40.
3. Trotsky, pp 28 ff. Even when Trotsky's political predictions were incorrect this work, first published in 1926, provided the keenest insight into the decline of the British economy.
4. Marwick, p 64.
5. *The Triumph of Nationalisation* quotedin *Westralian Worker*, 11 September.
6. Aldcroft, p 13.
7. Dutt, 'The Capitalist Offensive in Britain', reprinted in Australian Worker, 21 October.
8. Extract from the address by A B Swales to the TUC conference, reprinted in *Worker's Weekly*, 11 September.
9. Rates of dividends were taken by Dutt from the Economist.
10. Pollard, p 47.
11. *Ibid*, pp 48–49.
12. *Ibid*, pp 67–68.
13. Pollard, pp 118, 154.
14. This was partly offset by an increase in first class traffic during this period.

15. The Canadian government appointed Preston to inquire into the operation of the shipping lines and their effect on the country. The Report was quoted in *Australian Worker*, 26 August and *New Zealand Worker*, 7 October.
16. *Westralian Worker*, 28 August, 4 and 11 September.
17. *Westralian Worker*, 21 October, quoted Inchcape as saying in evidence that 'It would be very hard if there was an Act compelling the shipping companies to disclose their profits to the Imperial Shipping Committee'.
18. Quoted in *Australian Worker*, 11 November.
19. See chapter 2.

The Seafarers and their Organization, pp 13–26

1. According to the leaked 'Minutes of Proceedings . . . on June 28th, 1925 . . .'
2. But see below for the way the wage increase was arranged.
3. Thanks to the Shipping Federation (now the Chamber of Shipping) for providing access to their minute book.
4. There are many gaps in the papers of the NSFU, deposited at the Modern Records Centre, University of Warwick and very little on the strike of 1925. A copy of the letter referred to here was not found.
5. Mogridge provides a useful review article.
6. Short-lived seamen's combinations extend back to 1810. For a brief account see the Webbs, fn, p 392.
7. Powell, pp 5–6.
8. In Rotterdam there was a surplus of labour available, but in Amsterdam twenty out of thirty-five ships were strike bound and cavalry and police were used to break the strike.
9. For the accompanying race riots see chapter 4.
10. Mogridge.
11. Holton, p 90.
12. See Evans (1988b). Tupper's role is discussed below.
13. See chapter 4 for another side to the events of 1911.
14. Mogridge.
15. See Mogridge. In 1894 after the union went bankrupt. The reconstituted NSFU abolished local branch autonomy (under which funds had been frittered away) and money was centrally controlled.
16. Shinwell (1981), p 48.
17. *Ibid*, pp 54–5.
18. Chatham, p 68.
19. See letter from Wilson to Sir Thomas Royden, January 1926, Liverpool University Archives, Cunard, D.42.C2/255. Lindop says that opposition members were suspended, expelled, or bought off.
20. Lindop, ch 10.

21. *Marine Worker*, August.
22. Amalgamated Marine Workers' Union, *PC5*, p 10.
23. Meeting of the AMWU held in Antwerp; MSS 175/6/AMW/4/8, MRC.
24. Congress of Seamen's Section of the International Transport Workers' Federation, MSS 159/1/5/5, MRC.
25. Mogridge, p 400.
26. Report signed by J Hamans, Mss 175/6/AMW/4/19, MRC.
27. See AMWU minutes and proceedings of meetings, 8/9 June 1925: General Executive Council, MSS 175/6/AMW/4/21, MRC.
28. Fittingly, this was written in a foreword for his 'good friend's' [Wilson's] autobiography on 25 July 1925.
29. Bullock, p 411.
30. *Marine Worker*, January 1922, quoted by Chatham, p 68.
31. Maritime Joint Commission report, International Labour Bureau, League of Nations, Paris 8–10 March 1922, Mss 175/3/11/1 MRC. The money was ostensible for the families of seamen killed during the war.
32. Printed at the back of Havelock Wilson, *The Red Hand Exploiting the Trade Union Movement.*
33. Reader's Letters, *Daily Record and Mail*, 25 September.

The Strike begins in Britain, pp 27–36

1. Jones, p 56.
2. Quoted at the head of Chapter 1.
3. Calhoun, p 172, estimated the range as 13–48 per cent.
4. Calhoun, pp 172–3.
5. Maurice Hankey, Permanent Secretary to the Cabinet, letter to the King, quoted by Farman, p 43.
6. *Weekly Worker*, 7 August.
7. Statement of aims: outlined by A Lozovsky at the Fourth Congress of the Comintern, November 1922, quoted in Hinton and Hyman, p 24.
8. Calhoun, p 66 ff.
9. Hardy, *passim*, was one of the few participants who wrote an account of the strike.
10. See report of formation of the seamen's section, *Workers Weekly*, 17 July 1924.
11. *Hull Evening News*, 1 August; *North Mail and Newcastle Chronicle*, 1 August.
12. The *Southern Daily Echo*, 17 August, reported that ships were held up in Hull and London. The *North Mail and Newcastle Chronicle*, 18 August, denied this but said that the strike had spread to Newcastle.
13. *International Press Correspondence (Inprecor)*, organ of the Communist International, 29 October.
14. *Daily Herald*, 17 August.

15. *Ibid*; *Evening News*, 20 August.

16. *Liverpool Post*, 20 August.

17. See eg *Daily Herald*, 22 August.

18. Reports from *Daily Record and Mail*, 25, 26 August; *Evening News*, 25 August; *Evening Citizen*, 25 August; *Southern Daily Record*, 25 August; University Liverpool Archives D.42.C2/255. By way of contrast, the *Journal of Commerce*, which predicted the end of the strike weekly, said on 25 August that 'one or two ships here and there were temporarily delayed ...'

19. There was a history of gun carrying on the water front, and in some regions union officials were known to be armed.

20. Both the shooting and the trial were widely reported in the press: the affray on 27, 28 August, and the trial on 17 and 18 September.

21. Tupper, p 274. Even if the story is subjected to the same doubt as all Tupper stories, the attitude reflects the conditions of the time.

22. *Southern Daily Echo*, 31 August.

23. R E Bond, writing in *Inprecor*, only mentions the AMWU to condemn it for splitting the ranks of the seamen. Although some of his criticisms of this union must be taken seriously (see below) the denial of any positive role to the AMWU is absurd.

24. For an account of the tugmen, see below. Shinwell omits any reference to the 1925 strike in the many versions of his memoirs. He did not answer our letters with questions on this event.

25. But even this would leave unexplained the delay until the end of August.

26. *Daily Record and Mail*, 3 September.

27. *Daily Herald*, 3 September.

28. Memorandum from Manager's office to Chairman, 24 August 1925, University of Liverpool Archives, Cunard D.42.C2/255.

29. Copies of the bulletins have not been found. Issue, No 9 is reprinted in *The Seaman*, 25 September, organ of the NSFU.

30. Hardy, p 178.

31. From the context it was obvious that Laws meant Shinwell. The minutes inadvertently named Wilson as the person concerned!

32. See chapter 10 for the strike by the wireless operators.

Racism and the Sailors, pp 37–42

1. From a nine point programme printed in the *Marine Worker*.

2. *Forward*, 11 April 1914. Our stress.

3. Hardy (1927) said that in 1926 51,566 Lascars worked on British ships: 6,500 of them in mixed crews, the others on uni-racial ships. They were paid less than £2 per month and the food was 'uneatable', p 15.

4. *Westralian Worker*, 18 September.

5. *Ibid*, 30 October.

6. It is embarrassing to have to show that Lascars took strike action to improve their wages and work conditions. On 2 September the *Daily Record and Mail* reported that 3,000 Lascars employed by the Irrawaddy Flotilla Company were striking for an increase of wages. They were replaced by scabs! That presumably shows that some (Lascars?) could not be relied upon.

7. Our thanks to Neil Evans (1988a,b) for information on conditions in Cardiff.

8. Locally resident Chinese employed on British ships under British articles were paid 75 per cent of the going rate. Chinese scabs were paid at the appreciably lower Hong Kong rates.

9. We quote reluctantly. Tupper was a disreputable story teller. His story of 'little white girls' was part of the standard racism of the time.

10. Foot, pp 103 ff.

11. Sir Ernest Wylde, (*Hansard*, 15 April 1919), quoted by Foot, p 105.

12. Gordon and Reilly, p 76.

13. William P Samuels, quoted by Fryer, p 298.

14. See May and Cohen.

15. Evans (1985), p 78.

16. *Ibid*, p 77.

17. Gordon and Reilly.

18. Nonetheless a photograph of the strike committee in New Zealand (sent us by Bert Roth) has one member who is black.

Solidarity Abroad, pp 43–50

1. A paper owned by the right–wing Australian Workers Union.

2. Minutebook of the South Australian Branch of the Federated Seamen's Union.

3. *Ibid*, 20 August.

4. *Australasian Seamen's Journal*, Vol 8, No 53.

5. Mr Raeburn, secretary of the Australian seamen's union, who had been contacted by the Adelaide branch, writing in the Sydney Labour Daily and quoted in *New Zealand Worker*, 9 September.

6. According to the *Daily Record and Mail*, 27 August.

7. Letter from Millars' Timber and Trading Co, Perth, agents for the SA government, to the Premier [P Collier of the ALP], 24/8/25, Acc 1496, AN 2/1, Premier's Dept, Shipping Strike 1925, Vol III, No 122. Kindly sent us by P Gifford.

.8. *Daily Record and Mail*, 27 August.

9. *Australia's Heritage*, Vol 16, p 1821; Morris.

10. Morris; Farrell, pp 53, 62.

11. Victorian Socialist Party circular: 'The Seamen's Fight', 18 July 1925.

12. Fitzpatrick and Cahill, p 58. The deregistration continued over ten years.

13. *Debates*: Australian Senate, 1925, pp 1008-1090, and House of Representatives, pp 1090–1275. The debates started at 3 .00 pm on Wednesday 15 July in the Senate, and concluded at 7.02 am on Friday 17 July in the lower house.
14. *Debates,* pp 1236–8.
15. *Ibid*, pp 1074–5.
16. See Farrell, pp 8–9, 15–7, 88–9.
17. *Debates*, p 1057
18. *Ibid*, pp 1030–31. Other representatives, although less strident did not repudiated these views. The most heated slanging match in the Senate occurred when members accused each other of wishing to introduce more Chinese into the country. (See e.g. Foll vs. McHugh, p 1070).
19. *Ibid*.
20. *Australia's Heritage*; *Daily Herald*, 1 August 1925.
21. *Star*, 24, 26 August; *Argus*, and *Natal Advertiser*, 28 August.
22. Under the (British) Merchant Shipping Act of 1894, the withdrawal of labour in the merchant marine, anywhere in the world and wherever it could be enforced, was an offence at all times.
23. *Natal Mercury*, 28 August. Returned in the elections of June 1924 with 63 Nationalists and 18 members of the SALP.
24. One boat stopped in Lourenco Marques and one in East London. Newspapers said the strike lasted 47 days but many ships were held up for 60 days or more.
25. Letter from Millars Timber and Trading Co, *op cit*, No 124.
26. *Natal Advertiser*, 1 September.
27. Simons and Simons, p 229.
28. *Umteteli wa Bantu*, 10 May 1925.
29. Quoted in *Natal Advertiser*, 2 September. Escombe intervened to prevent disorder at the Point in 1897, following public agitation against the continued importation of indentured Indian labour.
30. For Simons's activities see:*Rand Daily Mail*, 29 May 1913–3 June 1913; *Transvaal Leader*, 18, 31 January 1914. The 18 January report says Simons intervened at a Benoni meeting to stop a Vigilance Committee being formed and secured support for the railwaymen's strike.
31. *Natal Mercury*, 2, 3 September. None of the reports we saw referred to Kemp's or Simons's past political affiliations or activities.
32 Duncan, a minister in the Smuts government was later Governor-General of South Africa. Dr Malan led the Nationalist government in 1948.
33. *Natal Mercury,* 4 September.
34. *Ibid*, 2 September; *Times of India*, 2, 3 September.
35. *Natal Mercury*, 2 September.
36. *Ibid*, 3 September.
37. *Natal Advertiser*, 3 September; *Times of India*, 4 September (which inserted the words that had been excluded to cut the cost of cabling).

38. Reports appeared in *Times of India*, 1–5 September, and in the press in South African, Britain and Australia — some came via Reuters, others without reference to any news agency.
39. Quoted in *Star*, 2 September.
40. Letter from General Hertzog to Mayor of Durban, reported in *Natal Mercury*, 3 September; *Times of India*, 4 September.

All Out in Australia, pp 51–63

1. *Argus*, 22 August.
2. *Australian Worker*, 26 August.
3. The extracts, and reply by the union, quoted in *Australasian Seamen's Journal*, 20 August.
4. *Evening Post*, 23 August.
5. *Argus*, 24 August.
6. *Australian Worker*, 26 August.
7. *Argus*, 24 August.
8. *Australian Worker*, 26 August.
9. *Ibid*.
10. *Daily Record and Mail*, 31 August.
11 Carment, p 49.
12. *Ibid*, pp 52–3.
13. *Argus*, 25 August.
14. *Argus*, 31 August.
15. *Daily Record and Mail*, 2 September.
16. *Leader*, 12 September.
17. B Walker, p 249.
18. *Sydney Morning Herald*, 12 September. It seems likely that it was the same event (somewhat sensationalised) that appeared a week later in the *Leader* under banner headlines: 'Sensational Arrests in Sydney', in which it reported violent clashes following a police raid at the railway cafe to arrest striking seamen. An armed policeman held back the crowd while seamen were taken away.
19. The minutes of the Adelaide branch of the FSU has no news of the arrests.
20. Johnson was a member of the Australian Socialist Party: a small group that proclaimed that revolutionaries could only take political power when they had the whole-hearted support of the masses.
21. *Sydney Morning Herald*, 22 October.
22. *Australian Worker*, 21 October.
23. *Ibid*, 7 October.
24. B Walker, pp 244–9.
25. See *Westralian Worker*, 2 October.

26. Letter to Joseph Morris, General Secretary, WWFofA, 15 September. These are included in documents held by the Archives of Business and Labour, Australian National University, file no T62/28/9.
27. Henry Earnest Boote, described as 'not really of the left although he was a leader in the fight against conscription and in defending victimised Wobblies — basically a civil libertarian'. (Letter from P Gifford, 1 May 1991)
28. *Leader*, 26 September.
29. *Australian Worker*, 21 October.
30. *Sydney Morning Herald*, 26 October.
31. 130 from Bowen, about 100 from Ayr and 50 from Proserpine.
32. *Sydney Morning Herald*, 4 November.
33. This paragraph is compiled from reports in the *Sydney Morning Herald*, 2–4 November.
34. *Sydney Morning Herald*, 7 November.
35. *Leader*, 3 October.
36. *Daily Record and Mail*, 3 October.
37. L Rees, pp 26–7. Our thanks to Rowan Cahill for a copy of this account.
38. Report of W C Sellinger, Inspector of Police, to Police Commissioner R Connell, 30 November 1925, Fremantle DPO, No 2018, 1925, General File 6751/25. Thanks to P Gifford for sending us this copy.
39. *Westralian Worker*, 13 November.

The Strike in South Africa, pp 64–71

1. *Times*, 6 November.
2. *Evening News*, 1 September.
3. *Daily Dispatch*, 10 September.
4. *Natal Advertiser*, 26 August.
5. *Star*, 3 September.
6. Quoted in *Natal Witness*, 29 August.
7. In 1928 S P Bunting, the party leader, complained in Moscow that in 1925 the CPSA had received no communication on the strike from abroad.
8. *Evening Citizen*, 31 August; *Friend*, 31 August.
9. *Cape Argus*, 2 September. Berman, one-time editor of the *Bolshevik* in Cape Town, was a member of the SALP.
10. *Daily Record and Mail*, 4 September.
11. *Star*, 4 September.
12. Biurski. Newspaper reports confirm much of Biurski's account. In the event of discrepancies we have quoted from the press.
13. South African Department of Justice files 3/1064/18, Report to Secretary for Justice, 1 February 1926. Also statement by a fireman in *Cape Argus*, 5 Septem-

ber: 'We are not Communists — but they are the only ones collecting money for us in order to send cables and wires and they offered us their hall to meet in.'

14. *Cape Argus*, 23 September.

15. *Evening News*, 1 September; *Star*, 2 September.

16. *Star*, 3 September.

17. *Cape Argus*, 4 September.

18. Biurski, p.36; *Daily Dispatch*, 9 September.

19. *Star*, 9 September; *Fairplay*, 25 September.

20. *Daily Record and Mail*, 9 October.

21. *Star*, 17, 22 September.

22. *Daily Record and Mail*, 22 September.

23. *Star*, 5 September; *Natal Mercury*, 9 September. A Department of Labour dispatch suggested that the wage cut be postponed for six months and that the unions be adequately represented on the NMB, or that this be investigated at a top level British inquiry; see *Daily Dispatch*, 9 September.

24. Roe quotes one prurient observer as saying life aboard ship was 'perhaps beyond the norms of ship-board liberation'.

25. *Natal Mercury*, 7 September. Biurski, p 35, states that the crew used semaphore to signal that the officers were firing the boilers and he had suggested this course of action.

26. *Natal Mercury*, 11 September.

27. The first attempt to take a ship out with the crew held below board was in Cape Town (see below). See *Natal Mercury*, 10 September; *Star*, 19 September; *Daily Record and Mail*, 8 September.

28. Telegram, 18 September 1925, Central Archives, Pretoria: Justice File, 409:4/385/25 part 2.

29. *Star*, 19, 24 September. The latter report said that the Johannesburg branch of the ICU was forwarding £3 5s 6d to the strikers, with a pledge of more to come.

30. *Daily Record and Mail*, 8 September.

31. Strike Bulletin No 9 (reprinted in *Natal Advertiser*, 25 September) reporting on imprisoned strikers: said only one ship had left South Africa for Britain, and that some ships with scab crews had left 'home ports' but few had returned.

32. *Natal Advertiser*, 29 September, reprinted the latest strike bulletin and carried reports of pickets.

33. *Cape Argus*, 16 September.

34. See *Natal Mercury*, 22 September, on the defiant response of 120 scabs on the *Arundel Castle* to the strikers appeal.

35. Reported in the *Southern Daily Echo*, 28 September.

36. *Natal Mercury*, 31 August.

37. *Cape Argus*, 7 September.

38. The fullest account appeared in the *Natal Advertiser*, 8 September.

39. See *Cape Argus*, 17 September. The Cape Town Tramway Union donated £400; the Typographical Union called for a voluntary levy of 1s per man per week; the Carpenters Union resolved to discuss the matter.

40. *Cape Argus*, 24 September.

41. *Natal Mercury*, 28 September.

42. *Cape Argus*, 1 October.

43. See *Daily Record and Mail*, 22 September, for a gloomy assessment of the economic situation in South Africa.

44. *Natal Mercury*, 1 October.

45. *Cape Argus*, 12 October. The International Transport Workers Federation, *Press Report*, No 22, 24 October, said the number of votes against was 240.

46. ITWF *Press Report*, No.22, 24 October; No 23: 7 November.

47. *Workers Weekly*, 4 December.

48. *Natal Mercury*, 24 September.

49. This will appear in Hirson's biography of Frank Glass.

50. The Alpers were known for their socialist activities: first in Pretoria, as members of the International Socialist League, then in Durban as supporters of the left. A letter in the *Natal Advertiser*, 21 September, accused Minnie Alper of being a fomenter of the strike, and an editorial condemned her as an 'unabashed Communist'.

51. Kentridge wrote articles on the strike putting the case for higher wages in *Forward*. There was no reply from the Creswell camp.

The 'Homeboat' Strike, pp 72–80

1. The sequence of events in New Zealand was pieced together from the available press items. These are far from full and further research might reveal a more complex account.

2. Henceforth 'New Zealand' when used in titles of newspapers will be written as 'NZ'.

3. *Argus*, 25 August.

4. *NZ Times*, 25 August.

5. Bollinger, pp 154–5 says that the *NZ Worker* gave full-hearted support to the strike. The New Zealand seamen's union had an investment in the the*Worker* (as it was popularly known) but the paper was not uncritical of the union and clashed with Walsh and Butler — see below.

6. Bollinger, p 155.

7. *NZ Transport Worker*, 1 October 1925.

8. Printed 'Statement of Receipts and Payments', 1 September 1925 to 14 January 1926.

9. Details of charges, and sentences appeared in *NZ Worker*, 16 September. The number of men affected was not given.

10. Quoting from Christopher Addison, *Politics from Within*.

11. *Round Table*, March 1926.
12. *Daily Record and Mail*, 30 September.
13. Details from P M Butler's letter (1984), *op cit*.
14. *Fairplay*, 15 October.
15. Several documents quoted in this chapter are from the Alexander Turnbull Library, Wellington. These proved invaluable in piecing together this account.
16. *Round Table*, 26 March.
17. *Auckland Star*, 26 October.
18. *Star*, Christchurch, 10 October.
19. Thanks to Viv Porzsolt who sent us the relevant portion of this mimeographed document.
20. *NZ Transport Worker*, 1 November.
21. Report, 'New Zealand Waterside Workers', *op cit*.
22. Report of Secretary, *op cit*.

The Strike Grinds Down, pp 81–89

1. *Liverpool Post and Mercury*, 5 September.
2. *Daily Herald*, 5 September. Our emphasis.
3. *North Mail and Newcastle Chronicle*, 3 September.
4. *Daily Herald*, 8, 9 September.
5. *North Mail and Newcastle Chronicle*, 9 September. The reeport derided Shinwell's attempts to get the strike discussed. Shinwell does not refer in his memoirs to the events at the conference.
6. See statement by M E Boggin below.
7. *Workers Weekly*, 11 September.
8. *Daily Herald*, 16, 18 September.
9. *Daily Record and Mail*, 19 September.
10. *Daily Herald*, 5 September.
11. *Daily Record and Mail*, 19 September.
12. *Southern Daily Echo*, 18 September. This is an area that requires further research. We found only a few letters from women in the British press on this subject.
13. *Daily Record and Mail*, 4 September.
14. *Daily Courier* and *Liverpool Post and Mercury*, 14–16 September.
15. *Daily Courier*, 22, 23 September.
16. *Daily Courier*, 24 September.
17. *Daily Herald*, 9 September. This report was from Hull, but the practice was undoubtedly the same elsewhere.
18. *Southern Daily Echo*, 11 September.
19. *Ibid*, 18 September. See also report on the strike in *Marine Worker*, October 1925.

20. *Daily Courier*, 16 September.
21. *Southern Daily Echo*, 2 October. The reports cover attacks on individuals, crowd action and also incidents in which pickets were charged after peacefully persuading men not to scab.
22. *Daily Echo*, 8 September.
23. Reprinted in International Transport Worker's Federation *Press Report*, No 22, 24 October 1924.
24. *Southern Daily Record*, 12 October.
25. *Hampshire Advertiser and Independent*, 16 October.
26. *Daily Herald*, 14 October.
27. *Workers Weekly*, 23 October.
28. Labour Research Department, p 46 ff.
29. This is discussed in *Westralian Worker*, 4 December.

Strike Against the Tide, pp 90–93

1. A survey of industrial action by seamen by Jack Kinahan, a research officer with the National Union of Seamen, in 1976, failed to mention the strike of 1925. His article, 'Maritime industrial relations: concepts and consequences', printed in *Maritime Policy Management*, is cited by P Gifford, p 64.
2. *Sunday Worker*, 18 October
3. Klugman does not mention the strike in the official party history, nor does Harry Pollitt (the leader of the NMM) in his autobiography.
4. *Daily Record and Mail*, 2 October.
5 *Westralian Worker*, 16 October, commenting on a letter by Havelock Wilson to Australian trade unionists in September.
6 Farman, pp 60–64; Calhoun, p 229; Klugman, pp 36–9.
7 Letter from AMWU to the ITWU, 12 January 1926. Copy at MRC.
8. National Union of Seamen, p 22.
9. Mogridge, p 407; Farman, p 259.
10. Letter to Walter Citrine of the TUC dated 10 May 1926, signed by Edo Fimmen, Secretary of the ITF. Telegrams sent by Wilson to Fimmen are prize examples of Wilson's rudeness. Copies at MRC.
11. See Chapter 2.

BIBLIOGRAPHY

Primary Sources

Archives of Business and Labour, Australian National University.
Biurski, Solomon (nd), 'Fleeting Memories' (Typescript).
Bollinger, Conrad, MS Papers (Alexander Turnbull Library, Wellington).
Borlase, J (nd), Typescript on NSFU, Modern Records Centre (MRC), University of Warwick.
The Chamber of Shipping (formerly the Shipping Federation), Minute Book.
'Congress of the Seamen's Section of the International Transport Workers Federation, May 1923', MRC, University of Warwick, Mss 159/1/5/5.
Debates: Federal Senate and House of Representatives, Australia, 1925.
International Federation of Trade Unions, Report on Activities During the Years 1924/25/26, Amsterdam, 1927.
International Transport Workers Federation, Papers, MRC.
National Maritime Board, Minutes of Meetings: Sailors and Fireman's Board; Full Board.
National Sailors and Fireman's Union of Great Britain and Ireland, (1925), 'Minutes of Proceedings of a Conference, re Wages'.
—— Minute Book, (MRC).
New Zealand Waterside Workers' Federation, Report of Secretary, 1925.
Shipping Federation, Minutes of Legal and Indemnity Committee.
—— Minutes of Proceedings of Executive Council, 1924/1925.
Trades Union Congress (TUC) Annual Reports, 1925–26.

Correspondence with and/or Assistance from

Beinart, William (Bristol); Broeze, Frank (Nedlands, WA); Bruce, David (Watford); Butler, P M (Upper Hutt, NZ); Cahill, Rowan (Bowral, NSW); Davin, Anna (London); Evans, Bob (Melbourne); Farrell, Frank (Kensington, NSW); Ghazi-Horsiny, Clare (London); Gifford, Peter (Attadale, WA); Gill, Tom (Melbourne); Higgs, Denis (Ontario); Hirson, Allen (London); Kaminer, Bob and Renate (Melbourne); Lambert, Rob (Durban); Marsh, A I (Oxford); Page, Martin (London); Porzsolt, Viv (New Zealand); Roe, Michael (Hobart); Roth, Bert (Auckland); Singleton, Patrick (Melbourne); Trewhela, Paul (Aylesbury).

Libraries
Alexander Turnbull Library (Wellington); Australian National Library (Canberra); British Library (London); Durban Municipal Library; Institute of

Commonwealth Studies (London); State Library of Victoria (Melbourne): University of Liverpool Archives; University of Warwick (Coventry), MRC.

Newspapers (towns/cities are indicated only where the location might not be obvious)

Great Britain
Daily Courier (Liverpool)
Daily Herald (London)
Daily Record and Mail (Glasgow)
East London Observer (London)
Evening Citizen (Glasgow)
Evening News (Glasgow)
Fairplay (London)
Forward (Glasgow)
Glasgow Evening News
Glsgow Evening Standard
Hampshire Advertiser and Independent (Southampton)
Hull Evening News
Journal of Commerce (Liverpool)
Liverpool Post and Mercury
Marine Worker (London)
Northern Mail and Newcastle Chronicle
Plebs
Round Table (London)
Seaman
Southern Daily Echo (Southampton)
Sunday Worker (London)
Times (London)
Worker s' Weekly (London)
The Worker (NMM) (Glasgow)

New Zealand
Auckland Star
Evening Post
New Zealand Times (Wellington)
New Zealand Transport Worker (Wellington)

New Zealand Worker (Wellington)
Star (Christchurch)

South Africa
Cape Argus (Cape Town)
Cape Times (Cape Town)
Daily Dispatch (East London)
Forward (Johannesburg)
Friend (Bloemfontein)
Natal Advertiser
Natal Mercury (Durban)
Star (Johannesburg)
Transvaal Leader (Johannesburg)
Umteteli wa Bantu

Australia
Australian Worker (Sydney)
Leader (Melbourne)
Queensland Industrial Gazette (Brisbane)
Sydney Morning Herald
Westralian Worker (Perth)
Worker (Brisbane)
Workers Weekly (Sydney)

Europe and Elsewhere
Canadian Labour World (Hamilton, Ontario)
International Press Correspondence (Inprecor)
International Transport Workers Federation Press Report
Times of India

SECONDARY SOURCES

Aldcroft, Derek H (1977), *From Versailles to Wall Street, 1919–29*, Allen Lane.

Amalgamated Marine Workers Union (1922), *PC5: J Havelock Wilson's Attempt to Enslave British Seamen Exposed.* Verbatim Report of an Extraordinary Meeting Held at the National Sailors' and Firemen's Union, Head Office, April 23rd, 1922.

—— (1925), 'Seamen's Dispute: The Conspiracy Exposed. How the Seamen's Wages were Reduced'.

Anon (1971), *Australia's Heritage: The Making of a Nation*, Vol 16, Hamlyn, Sydney.

Ashworth, T R (nd), *The Story of the Unofficial Strike of Seamen in Australia was a Communist Plot to Destroy the British National Union of Seamen*.

Atchkanov, G (1927), *Havelock Wilson Exposed*, Seamen's Section of the Transport Workers Minority Movement.

Bell, Thomas (1937), *The British Communist Party: A Short History*, Lawrence and Wishart.

Bollinger, Conrad (1968), *Against the Wind: The Story of the New Zealand Seamen's Union*, Reed, Wellington.

Bond, R E (1925), 'The Unofficial Strike of British Seamen', *Inprecor*, Vol 5, No 77.

Bullock, Alan (1960), *The Life and Times of Ernest Bevin*, Vol 1, Heinemann.

Burley, Kevin (1968), *British Shipping and Australia, 1920–39*, Cambridge University Press.

Calhoun, David F (1976), *The United Front: The TUC and the Russians, 1923–28*, Cambridge University Press.

Carment, David (1977), 'Sir Littleton Groom and the Deportation Crisis of 1925: A Study of Non-Labour Responses to Trade Union Militancy', *Labour History,*, No 32, May.

Chatham, John (1981), 'British Seafarers: The Opposition to Collaboration, 1911 to 1927', Unpublished MA, University of Warwick.

Clark, David (1985), *Victor Grayson, Labour's Lost Leader*, Quartet.

Clegg, Hugh Armstrong (1985), *A History of British Trade Unionism Since 1889*, Vol 2, Clarendon.

Cole, G D H and Postgate, Raymond (1961), *The Common People*, Methuen

Cowling, Maurice (1971), *The Impact of Labour, 1920–1924*, Cambridge.

Creswell, Margaret (nd), *An Epoch of the Political History of South Africa in the Life of Frederick Hugh Page Creswell*, Balkema, Cape Town.

Edward, Cecil (1965), *Bruce of Melbourne: Man of Two Worlds*, Heinemann.

Evans, Neil (1980), 'The South Wales Race Riots of 1919', *Llafur: The Journal of the Society for the Study of Welsh Labour History*, Vol 3, No 1, Spring.

—— (1980), 'Regulating the Reserve Army: Arabs, Blacks and the Local State in Cardiff, 1919–45', in Kenneth Lunn.

—— (1988a), 'Civil War in "Darker Cardiff"', typescript.

—— (1988b), '"A Tidal Wave of Impatience": The Cardiff General Strike of 1911', typescript.

Farman, C (1972), *May 1926: The General Strike*, Panther.

Farrell, Frank (1981), *International Socialism and Australian Labour: The Left in Australia, 1919–39*, Hale and Iremonger, Sydney.

Fitzpatrick, Brian and Cahill, Rowan J (1981), *The Seamen's Union of Australia: 1872–1972*, Seamen's Union of Australia, Sydney.

Foot, Paul (1965), *Immigration and Race in British Politics*, Penguin.

Fryer, Peter (1984), *Staying Power: the History of Black People in Britain*, Pluto.

Gallagher, William (1948), *Revolt on the Clyde*, Lawrence and Wishart.

Gifford, Peter (1991), 'No Winners, the British Seamen's Strike of 1925 – Its Ramifications at Home and in the Commonwealth', BA (Hons) dissertation, Murdoch University.

Gordon, Paul and Reilly, Danny (1986), 'Guestworkers of the Sea: Racism in British Shipping', *Race and Class*, Vol 28, No 2.

Hardy, George (1927), *The Struggle of British Seamen*, Published by Seamen's Section of Transport Workers Minority Movement for the International Propaganda Committee of Transport Workers.

—— (1956), *Those Stormy Years: Memories of the Fight for Freedom on Five Continents*, Lawrence and Wishart.

Hinton, James and Hyman, Richard (1975), *Trade Unions and Revolution: The Industrial Politics of the early British Communist Party*, Pluto.

Hirson, Baruch and Vivian, Lorraine (1986), 'The Homeboat Strike of 1925: British Seamen and South African Community Reactions', Colloquium Paper, Institute of Commonwealth Studies, London.

Holmes, Colin (ed)(1978), *Hosts, Immigrants and Minorities in British Society*,

Holton, Bob (1976), *British Syndicalism, 1900–1914: Myths and Realities*, Pluto.

Jones, Gareth Steadman (1966), 'History in One Dimension', *New Left Review*, No 36, March-April.

Joshua, Harris and Wallace, Tina, with Booth, Heather (1983), *To Ride the Storm: The 1980 Bristol 'Riot' and the State*, Heinemann.

Klugmann, James (1980), *History of the Communist Party of Great Britain, Vol 2, The General Strike, 1925–1926*, Lawrence and Wishart.

Labour Research Department (c1923), *An Analysis of the Shipping Industry: Do Your Own Thinking, Some Facts Which Will Help You*, Published by the Association of Wireless and Cable Telegraphists, London.

Lindop, F J (1972), 'A History of Seamen's Trade Unionism to 1929', Unpublished MA thesis, London University.

—— (c1978), 'Seamen and Dockers Unofficial Trade Union Activity in the 1920s', Unpublished paper.

Lunn, Kenneth (ed)(1980), *Race and Labour in Twentieth-Century Britain*, Frank Cass.

Martin, Roderick (1969), *Communism and the British Trade Unions, 1924–33: A Study of the National Minority Movement*, Clarendon.

Marwick, Arthur (1968), *Britain in the Century of the Total War: War, Peace and Social Change, 1900–1967*, Bodley Head.

May, J P (1978), 'The Chinese in Britain, 1860–1914', in Colin Holmes (ed).

May, Roy and Cohen, Robin (1974), 'The Interaction between Race and Colonialism: A Case Study of the Liverpool Race Riots of 1919', *Race and Class*, Vol 16, No 2.

Middlemas, Keith (1979), *Politics in Industrial Society: The Experience of the British System Since 1914*, Andre Deutsch.

Mogridge, Basil (1961),'Militancy and Inter-Union Rivalries in British Shipping, 1911–1929', *International Review of Social History*, Vol 6, Pt 3.

Morris, Richard (1979), 'Mr Justice Higgins Scuppered: The 1919 Seamen's Strike', *Labour History*, No 37, November.

National Union of Seamen (1962), *The Story of the Seamen: A Short History of the NUS*, Published by the NUS.

Olssen, Erik (1985), 'The Seamen's Union and Industrial Militancy, 1908–13', *New Zealand Journal of History*, 19(1), April.

Pollard, Sidney (1963), *The Development of the British Economy, 1914–1950*, Arnold.

Powell, L H (1950), *The Shipping Federation: A History of the First Sixty Years, 1890–1950*, Published for the Federation, London.

Rees, Leslie (1982), *Hold Fast to Dreams: Fifty Years in Theatre, Radio, Television and Books*, Alternative Publishing Co-Operative, Sydney.

Rees, Trevor R (1964), *Australia in the Twentieth Century: A Short Political Guide*, Cheshire, Melbourne.

Roe, Michael (1987), 'Strike Bound in Cape Town, 1925: Responses Aboard an Australian Migrant Ship', *Labour History*, No 53, November.

Roth, Bert and Hammond, Jenny (1981), *Toil and Trouble: The Struggle for a Better Life in New Zealand*, Methuen, New Zealand.

Shinwell, Emanuel (1955), *Conflict Without Malice*, Odhams.

—— (1973), *I've Lived Through it All*, Gollancz.

—— (1981), *Lead With the Left: My First Ninety Six Years*, Cassell.

Simons, J H and R E (1969), *Class and Colour in South Africa, 1850–1950*, Penguin.

Trotsky, Leon (1973), *On Britain*, Pathfinder.

Tupper, Capt Edward (1938), *Seamen's Torch*, Hutchinson.

Vivian, Lorraine (1987), 'The Unofficial Seamen's Strike, 1925', MA Dissertation, University of Warwick.

Walker, Bertha (1972), *Solidarity Forever . . . A Part Story of the Life and Times of Percy Laidler — The First Quarter of a Century*, National Press, Melbourne.

Walker, Eric (1947), *History of South Africa*, Longmans, Green.

Webb, Sidney and Beatrice (1907), *History of Trade Unionism*, Longmans, Green.

Wilson, J Havelock (1925b), *My Stormy Voyage Through Life*, NSFU, London.

—— Cotter, Joseph and Rostron, Capt A H (1925a), 'Addresses on Board the *SS Mauretania*, New York, 20 September', No publisher given.

—— (nd), *The Red Hand Exploiting the Trade Union Movement: The Communist Offensive Against the British Empire*, Twentieth Century Press.

INDEX

ADDISON, Cristopher, 78

Aldcroft, D, 9

Alien's Registration Act , 40

Allen, F C, 15

Alliance of Labour , see New Zealand A of L

Allotment, 6, stoppage of, 32, 53, 83–85

Alper, Minney, 71, fn, 104

Amalgamated Marine Workers Union (AMWU), 1, 15, 34, 70, 81, 84, and the strike, 1,3, on NSFU, 7, formed, 20, and PC5, 21, 93, squabbles in, 22, tugboats, 22, 32, Hull branch, 30, enters 1926 strike, 32, cafe, 35, racism, 38, 42, at TUC conference, 82, pay for strikers, 85, consulted about ending the strike, 86–87, 90, demise of the AMWU, 92, General Strike, 92, fns, 95–98

Anderson, Sir Alan, 17

Andrews, W H, 70

Anglo-Russian trade union committee, 28, 91

Anstey, Frank, on shipping companies, 11, on Wilson's income, 24, on Navigation Act, 46

Apolda, see South Africa

Arab seamen, 13, 41, in 1919 riots, 40, in 1925, 86

Armstrong, H T, attacks shipowners, 77–78

Asian seamen, 38, 41

Association of Wireless and Cable Telegraphists, 1, see also Wireless operators

Astbury, Mr Justice, 92–93

Australia, 2, 4, news of walk out, 32, Shipping Federation on strike, 36, racism, 38, 42, the SS Inkum, 44–45, white Australia policy, 46–47, 93, Deportation Board, 47, the strike, 44, 51ff, number of seamen and ships out, 51–52, 58, support for strikers, 52, 56–57, agricultural produce and strike, 53–54, 60, defections, 54, talks on settlement, 54, 58–59, arrests, 55, insulating the seamen, 56, general election called, 58, conflict in Queensland, 59–60, tension in Fremantle, 60–62, end of strike, 61–62, fns, 99–102

Australian Shipping Board, 45

BALDWIN, Stanley, on wages, 7

Ballarat, see South Africa

Berman, A Z, 65–66

Bevin, Ernest, 85

Bhyat, Amod, 49

Biurski, Solomon, 65–66, 71, fns, 102–103

Black seamen, in the war, 41

Blue Union, 92

Board of Guardians, and the dole, 84

Board of Trade, 21

Boggin, M E, 84–85

Bolshevik Revolution, 8, 73, 75

Bond, R E, 30, fn, 100

B[oote], Henry Earnest, 58, 62, fn, 104

Booth, 92

Bramley, Fred, 83

Britain, seamen's strike of 1925, 1, 12, first announcements of, 29–30, committee formed, 30, in Southampton, 33, AMWU enters the strike, 33, end of strike in South Africa heralds end in Britain, 70, Board of Guardians, 84–85, the anti-strike forces, 87, first ship back from the Cape, 88, concerted attack on trade unionism, 92, see also under organizations and leading figures

British economy, 7, dividends in, 10, Leon Trotsky on, 8, Palme Dutt on, 9, wage cuts, 9, 1925 slump, 12

British Board of Trade, on radio operators, 88

British Merchant Fleet, sea power, 9, 10–12, effect of recession, 11

British Seafarers Union, 19–21

Bruce, S M, 38, 53, 57–58, 72, 89, see Navigation Act

Bullock, Alan, on Wilson, 23

Bunting, S P, Comintern's failure to assist, 6, declaration on strike, 65, fn, 102

Butler, P M, background and involvement in 1925, 75–76, called in by prime minister, 79, advises return, 79

CANADA, 11, 81
Cannon, A, 32, 81, why the AMWU supported strike, 33
Cape Federation of Trades, 65, 70
Cardiff, riots of 1911, 39
Cartel, see Shipping cartel/combine
Central Strike Committee, 29, 30, 35, 88, 90, anti-racism, 43, at TUC conference, 82; end of strike, 86, see alsoUnofficial strike committee
Chinese sailors, 1, 21, in riots, 39, and Tupper, 40–41, fns, 99, see also riots
Charlton, Matthew, 58
Churchill, Winston, Chancellor of the Exchequer and gold standard, 12
Citrine, Walter, 81
Coates, Gordon, hopes to mediate, 78–80
Cole, G D H and R Postgate, on Wilson, 24
Coloured crews, aloofness in strike, 52
Committee of Overseas Seamen (NZ), 4
Commonwealth shipping line, 46
Communist Party of Australia, 45, 54, 57
Communist Party of Great Britain, 9, on **Red Friday**, 28; 91; on affiliation to Labour Party, 28, raided by police, 91, fn, 106
Communist Party of New Zealand, 75
Communist Party of South Africa, 6, 65–66, 68, 70–71
Communists, assistance for strike, 6; communist 'plot', 73–74
Concannon, Col H, anti–strike statement, 34
Cooks and Stewards Union, 20, 92
Cost of strike, see Economic impact.
Cotter, Joe, 10, 18, 20–22, 33, racism, 41–42, on **Mauretania**, 82
Creswell, Col F, negotiates for South African government, 65–67; 71
Cross–Channel ferries, strike, 33

DALGLEISH, 15
Deportation Board, see Australia
Dole money, 84–6
Duncan, Patrick, 49, fn, 103
Durban Strike Committee, 49–51, 68
Dutt, Palme, on British economy, 9–10

ECONOMIC impact of strike, 2, Australia, 60–

63, 88, South Africa, 64, 66, 70–71, New Zealand, 78, totals, 88–90, Britain, 91
Evans, Neil, on Tupper and riots, 40, fns, 98

FASCISM (nazism), 26, 40, 89, 90
Federated Seamen's Union of Australia (FSU), 43, 45, 57, deregistered, 45–46, see also Australia and individual names
Ferries, see cross-channel ferries
Fields, H G B, 54
Findley, E, on Navigation Act, 46
First World War, 8, 71, aftermath, 9, shipping losses, 10, post-war boom, 11, Shinwell and Wilson as patriots, 19, seamen as heroes, 20
Forster, Lord, 53

GALLAGHER, William, on Wilson, 24
General Strike, 1926, 2, prelude to, 27, 75, fear of capitalist assault, 91, NSFU refuses to participate, 92–93, fn, 106
General Workers Union, 36
Germans, see xenophobia
Glass, Frank, 70
Gold standard, Britain, 12

HARDY, George, 28–29, efficient organizer, 37, attitude to NSFU, 92
Hart, Rev J S, on wages, 3
Hertzog, General James B, 67, reaction to Lscars, 50, 64, 68

IMMIGRATION Restriction Act (SA), 68
Inchcape, Lord, and P&O, 12, 38, 74, 78, writes obituary to Wilson, 94
India, reactions to recruiting Lascars, 51
Indian sailors, see Lascars.
Indians in South Africa, 48–50, 71
Industrial and Commercial Workers Union (ICU), 68, 69
Industrial Peace Union, 25, 93
Industrial Workers of the World, 28
Inkum, 43–44
International Shipping Federation, 19
International solidarity, 6
International Transport Workers Federation, 18, 21, on seamen and General Strike, 93

JOHNSON (Johannsen) Jacob, 44, 48, 53; 55, 57–58, 93, arrest of, 54, fn, 101
Jones, Gareth, on General Strike, 27

KARIM, Abdul, 50
Kadalie, Clements, 69
Kemp, H H, 48–50, 71
Kentridge, Morris, 65–66, 70–71
Kessack, J O, against Lascars, 37–38
King George V, informed of cabinet plans, 27, fn, 97
Klenerman, Fanny, 70

LABOUR Party, Australian, 54, on Navigation Act, 46–47. on end of strike, 61–62,British, o n **Red Friday**, 28, see South African Labour Party
Labour Research Department, on racism, 41
LaGuma, James, 69
Lang, J T, 53
Lascars, (Indian sailors) 1, 38, 41–42, 71, 76, plans for scabs in South Africa, 42, 48–50, 68, fns, 99
Laws, Cuthbert, on Wilson, 15, on progress of strike, 35–36
Liverpool , riots, 41, strike in, 30
Lozovsky, Soloman A, 29, 36, 82, fn, 97
Lusitania, 20

MCKEE, H H, chairman of strike support committee, 44
McKinley, J, 32, 81
Madeley, Walter, 65–66, 70–71, 72
Malan, D F, 49, fn, 103
Mann, Tom, 1911 strike, 18
Marine Worker, on the strike, 7
Mineowners (British), call for wage cuts in Britain, 7
Miner's Federation of Great Britain, 7, 27, 77, Shinwell's belief in miner's support, 82
Miners Industrial (Spencer) Union, financed by Wilson, 93
Mogridge, Basil, 19, fns, 98
Money, Sir Leo Chiozza, 9
Mussolini, Benito, see fascism

NATAL Indian Association, 51
Natal Indian Congress, 50
National Maritime Board (NMB), 14, 16, 20, 21, 22, 24, 29, 34, 41, 87, 93
National Minority Movement (NMM), unofficial strike committee, 2, end of strike, 2,, 87, formation, 21, 28, Red International of Trade Unions, 28, impending wage cut, 29, reports on strike, 30, on tugs, 32, follows Lozovsky, 35, at TUC conference, 82–83, raided by police, 91
National Party (SA), 2, 42, 49, 64
National Sailors' and Firemen's Union 1, 51, 81, 64, 91, June conference, 13–14, 17, launched, 17, 1911 strike, 18, split, 20, in NMB, 21, Vigilance Committee's claims, 20, finances, 25, lack of activities, 26–27, members on strike committee, 30, 32, racism, 40–41, and TUC, 82, 89, clashes with strikers, 85, General Strike, 92–93, fns, 96ff
National Transport Workers Federation, 18, 21
Navigation Act Bill, 45–47
Navigation Commission (Aus), 21
New Zealand, 2, 4, 32, strike in 44; the 'Homeboat' strike, 72ff, seamen state their complaints, 73, 76, defence by **NZ Worker**, 74–75, 77, number out in New Zealand, 75, 80, seamen charged, 77, support committee, 75–77, against racism, 76, economic impact on, 78–79, scabs recruited, 79, end of strike, 80, fns, 104
New Zealand Alliance of Labour, 75
New Zealand Waterside Workers Federation, 76, report on strike, 79–80

OGDEN, J E, 46
Olssen, Erik, on work conditions, 4–5, fn,95
Organization for the Maintenance of Supplies, 91

PARR, Sir James, 78
Patten, T R, **Empress of France**, 31
Pearce, Frank, 18, 46
Peninsula and Oriental Shipping (P&O), profits of, 12
Pick, Joe, 65
Poor Law relief, 3, 31, 85
Port Consultant's Card (PC5), 21–22, 30, 92, AMWU's own PC5, 23, 35, 88
Powell, L H, 17, 23
Powers, Mr Justice, calls for talks, 59
Preston, W T R, 11, fn, 98
Profintern, see RILU

RACISM, and riots in Britain, 5, 37–42, in Australia, 5, riots in Tyneside, 41, riots in ports, 39–41, demands for repatriation of aliens, 42, Australian Navigation Act, 46–8, white Australia policy, 47–48, racism in 1925 strike, 86, Tom Walsh supports white Australia policy, 94, see South Africa

Red Friday, 1, 6, 28

Red International of Labour Unions (RILU), and NMM, 28, policy on union unity, 29, 82, 91

Red scare, 34, strike condemned as communist plot, 72–73; **passim**

Reed, George, shooting incident, 31–32, fns, 98

Rees, Leslie, retrospective on Fremantle events, 60–61

Reeves (NZ), 8

Repatriation committees, 40

Riley, E, 47

Rochlin, S A, 65

Roman Star, see South Africa

Runciman, Sir Walter, 24, 36

SCABBING, 17–18, organized, 31–33, 35, **passim**

Scab on the Ocean Wave, 82

Scullin, J H, on hum–bug about British ship's losses, 56

Seamen, anti-NSFU, 22; conditions of service, 26, fragmentation of, 81

Seamen's Strike Relief Committee (SA), 70

Seamen's Union of New Zealand, 76

Seamens' wages, Britain, 2–3, 12, 20, 43, 54, 63, 74, 84, background to wage cut, 13, offer of wage cut, 1, 14–17, Europe, 14, 16,, Australia, 44–45

Seamen's work conditions, 4

Seaton, James, 84

Shaw Savil Company, 80

Shinwell, Emanuel, 1, on split, 19, as war time recruiter, 19, on PC5, 22, on impending wage cut, 23, speaks on strike, 32–33, target of anti–semitism, 34, appraisal by Laws, 36, and TUC 81–82, 89, confidence in miners, 81, fns, 98

Shipping Cartel, 2, 11, 90, W Preston on, 11, Frank Anstey on, 12

Shipping Federation, 15, 66, 81, Ulster District Committee, 15–16, opposition to union, 17, 19,in NMB, 21, on PC5, 21, discuss strike, 35–36, rejects AMWU, 92, General Strike, 92

Shipping strike, 1911, 10, 18, for 1925 strike see Australia, Britain, South Africa and New Zealand

Shipowners, and strike, 2, 67–68, wealth of, 9

Ship's stewards, in 1911 strike, 20

Simons, Dan, 71, president of Durban strike committee, 48–50, fn, 100

Sophocles, see South Africa

South Africa, 2, 32, Shipping Federation on strike in, 36, racism in, 38, 42, the **SS Apolda**, 44, 47, first walk-out and arrests, 44, 47, government response, 50, use of Lascars, 49–50, economic impact, 64–65, 72, National Party opposes strike, 65, the **Roman Star**, 65–66, the **Ballarat**, 66–67, the **Sophocles** tries to sail, 67, number of ships involved in South Africa, 67, conditions in port, 69, scabs and the end of the strike, 68–70, 86, fns, 102ff

South African Indian Congress, 51

South African Labour Party, 2, 42, 48–49, 65–68, 70–71

Southampton, as centre of strike, 33, Trades and Labour Council meeting to support seamen, 83, Emergency Shipyard Worker's Committee, 83; Plumbers' Society Conference, 83

Special Restrictions Order, 41

Steward's and Cook's Union, racism, 40

Stinnes, Hugo, 25

Stockholm Peace Conference, 24

Strike action, 1925, was the strike a provocation?, 90, for events see under Australia, Britain, New Zealand and South Africa

Stuart, Bob, 70

Syndicalism, 22, 41

TRADES Union Congress (TUC), and seamens' strike, 1, call for 1925 strike, 7, on unity in seamen's union, 22, and RILU 28, attempt to amalgamate NSFU and AMWU, 81, TUC congress, 81–83, and NSFU, 90, 92, General Strike, 27, 93

Transport and General Workers Union, 87, 93

Trotsky, Leon, on British economy, 8, 9, fn, 95

Tupper, 'Captain' Edward, 1911 strike, 18, breaks up meetings, 20, characteristics of, 25, organizing zcabs, 32, anti-Chinese riots, 39–40

Tugboats, 22, 32, ,not called out, 34–35

U–BOATS, 19

Ulster District Committee, 15–16
Union Castle Line, 48–50, 68
United States, demonstrations in ports, 86, trade unions support Wilson, 86
Unofficial strike committee, 2, 42

VIGILANCE committees, 21, 25

WAGES, see seamen's wages
Walsh, Finstan Patrick, 75, 79
Walsh, Tom, 44–45, 56, strike leader, 46, government opposition, 47, on British seamen, 51ff, arrest of, 54, invited to form union in Britain, 56, 'conspiracy' theory, 57, lambasted by CPA, 57, condemned in New Zealand, 72–74, joins with Wilson in support of Industrial Peace Union, 93
Waterside Worker's Federation, 57
Watts, Sir Frederick Shadworth, 16
Wilson, J Havelock, 1, 7, 33, 51, 64, 66, 76, 82, 83, 85, 89; 92–93, June conference, 13–21, launched union, 17, split in union, 19, anti–pacifist campaign and CBE 20, appraisals of, 23–24, finances of, 25, Industrial Peace Union, 25, 93, control of union, 26, General Strike, 27, 94, attacks Tom Walsh, 51–52, cable to Bruce, 72, as the ''honest'' victim', 72–74, on **Mauretania**, 82, General Strike, 92–93, finances Spencer union and expelled from TUC, 93, death of, 93–94, fns, 96–97
Wireless operators, 36, organization and strikes of, 87–88
Women in the strike, 6, 83–85, bag makers, 84, see also allotment
Woodfort, A C, 43–44
Wooten, Charles, caught in riot, 40
World War, see First World War

XENOPHOBIA, in Britain, 40

YELLOW 'peril', 37